Back when we were
GLAM!

"It was a brillant era, wasn't it? The last proper era, probably."

—Mickie Most

"I think rock should be tarted up, made into a prostitute, a parody of itself. It should be the clown, the Pierrot medium."

—David Bowie

"Our function really is to relieve adolescents of their ills, of all the mental cruelty that's been bestowed on them."

—David Johansen, New York Dolls

Glam!

Bowie, Bolan and the Glitter Rock Revolution

Barney Hoskyns

foreword by Todd Haynes

POCKET BOOKS

NewYork London Toronto Sydney Toyko Singapore

POCKET BOOKS, a division of Simon & Schuster Inc.
1230 Avenue of the Americas, New York, NY 10020

ISBN: 0-671-03440-5

First Pocket Books trade paperback printing December 1998

10 9 8 7 6 5 4 3 2 1

For my darling boy Nat

contents

photo credits

Unless otherwise indicated, the photographs in this book are by Mick Rock. These photographs are © Mick Rock, 1972, 1973, 1974, 1998.

Other photographers whose work is included in this book are as follows:

Keith Morris: colour photograph of Marc Bolan and black and white photograph of Marc Bolan and Mickey Finn on page 9 © Redferns.

Robert Ellis: photograph of Eno and Andy Mackay; photograph of Bryan Ferry © Robert Ellis Repfoto.

Bob Gruen: colour photograph of the New York Dolls; photograph of Alice Cooper; photograph of Kiss © Bob Gruen, courtesy of Star File Photo.

Gered Mankowitz: photograph of Jobriath © Gered Mankowitz.

Dave Ellis: photograph of Elton John © Redferns.

Dezo Hoffmann: black and white photograph of Marc Bolan on page 1 © Dezo Hoffmann courtesy of Rex Features Ltd.

Barry Wentzell: black and white photograph of Roxy Music on page 55 © Barrie Wentzell/Repfoto.

Jim Chambers: black and white Photograph of Rodney's English Disco on page 67 © Jim Chambers.

Cover of the first Roxy Music album © Virgin Records Ltd, courtesy of IE Music Ltd.

Photograph from *Velvet Goldmine* courtesy of Channel Four Films/Goldwyn Films.

Photograph from *A Clockwork Orange* courtesy of BFI Stills, Posters and Design © Warner Bros.

ta very much

My thanks to the following for their reminiscences and ruminations: Bryan Ferry, Brian Eno, Lou Reed, Tony Visconti, David Johansen, Nicky Chinn, Kim Fowley, Rodney Bingenheimer, Bebe Buell, Laurence Myers, Simon Puxley, David Enthoven, Tim Clark, Todd Haynes, Bob Gruen and Mick Rock. Past interviews on which I drew for the book include those with Iggy Pop, Pamela Des Barres, Brett Anderson and Nick Kent.

For assistance and suggestions, thanks to: Walter Donohue, Todd Haynes, Oren Moverman, Julian Alexander, Kirsten Romano, Tam Hoskyns, Peter Harlowe, Tom Butler, Debby Butler, Edward Helmore, Ben Fisher, Abba Rage, Gail Ann Dorsey, Rob Cochrane, Nic Harcourt, Tony Visconti, Darcy Meyers, Charmian Norman-Taylor, Bill Kemble, Brad Simpson, Jon Riley, Chris Carter, Sarah-Jane Adler, Esther Rinkoff, Calvin Hayes, Chris Heath, Phil Savage, Kate Simon, Harvey Kubernik, John Walker . . . and of course my wife, Victoria.

foreword

The slice of mascara. The lamé flash. The glistening bolt of cosmetic lightning. Bowie's face on the cover of *Aladdin Sane*. And suddenly, in a suburban record store somewhere in LA, I am aware of a dark chill running through my twelve-year-old body, some dangerous affirmation daring me somewhere I am not ready to go.

Growing up in the States, I basically missed glam rock. Mainstream America was far too hooked on sixties rock for its glam following to be much more than an underground affair. But as the decade ensued it would become apparent, even to those of us tucked away in the suburbs, that something was lurking in the shadows of popular music, something strange and intoxicating that seemed to defy classification. Suddenly there were whole new words being exhaled from the cherry-red lips of the smoker girls at school, a strange dialogue freshly brimming with *iggys*, *ziggys*, *bowies* and *bi*'s. That face on the cover of *Aladdin Sane* disturbed and fascinated me, and cast an eerie pall over the certitude of my looming sexual identity. (I didn't buy the record.)

It wasn't really until I was in college that I would learn how much of the music I'd come to love – Bowie, Roxy, Iggy, Reed – had all been part of this brief chapter in pop history, centred in London, the result of a unique blending of underground American rock with a distinctly English brand of camp theatricality and gender-bending. And for a brief time pop culture would proclaim that identities and sexualities were not stable things but quivery and costumed, and rock and roll would paint its face and turn the mirror around, inverting in the process everything in sight.

Musically, lyrically, and in its revolution of images, glam rock was nothing short of a camp attack on rock and roll. When Marc Bolan wore glitter under his eyes on *Top of the Pops*, when Bowie went down on Mick Ronson's guitar, when the androgynous became the bisexual, it was clearly aimed at the intense morality of sixties youth culture (and the homophobia and misogyny it concealed) – and no longer at the older generation. Quite the contrary, glam rock was obsessed with the past, and made it its mission to weave its references into a world that combined nostalgia with futurism, torch balladry with hard rock, ironic melancholy with shock value. The very inverse of punk, the shock of glitter was the shock of the feminine. From Bowie's skeletal swish to Iggy's hard-core masochism, glam rock imposed a fierce, unnatural femininity on the masculine traditions of rock. Sure, it was a pose. But in the rare tradition of Oscar Wilde, artists like Bryan Ferry and Bowie were able to elevate artifice and irony in their work without sacrificing emotion in their music. Above all, in its parade of self-styled androgens and alter-egos, and in its declaration of 'ch-ch-changes' as the defining aspect of teen experience, the glam era presented to the world a new and radically fluid model for sexual identity: no longer defined by its permanence, but the multi-coloured result of constant change and reinvention.

It couldn't last. The 1980s were on their way – and with them, an overall retreat from the kinds of socio-political inversions that made glam rock possible in the first place. With few exceptions, glam would ultimately fall through the cracks of pop-cultural memory, dispersed and absorbed by gay disco and straight heavy metal, and punctuated by Bowie and Lou Reed's apparent disavowals of their homosexual pasts. Glam rock would become inconsequential to a world of restored binaries and boundaries, a world of men and women, straights and gays, and nothing of real interest in between. I guess it's not surprising that during my several years of research for what would become *Velvet Goldmine* I could find no book, in or out of print, on the glitter era. Books on individual artists acknowledge the period at length, but there was nothing to single it out as a comprehensive cultural phenomenon, including and defining a broad network of artists. So although I can only take credit for my powers of persuasion, this book is a first attempt to fill a symptomatic gap in rock journalism by examining this hugely influential and long overlooked era of glitter and music.

Todd Haynes
New York, 1998

ten glam signatures

1 The squealingly high backing vocals on T. Rex and Sweet singles

2 The fat sustain of the Gibson Les Paul guitar, as played by Marc Bolan, Mick Ronson, Johnny Thunders and Mick Ralphs

3 The compressed, mechanical drum sound that dominated glam pop from T. Rex to Suzi Quatro

4 The wide lapels of the satin jackets Marc Bolan wore on *Top of the Pops*

5 The orange 'mullet' sported by Ziggy Stardust

6 The *faux*-cockney vibrato of David Bowie, Ian Hunter, Steve Harley, Brett Anderson et al

7 The giant silver platforms worn by Iggy Pop, Gary Glitter and others

8 The chamber-rock arrangements of Tony Visconti and Mick Ronson (T. Rex, Bowie), Bob Ezrin (Alice Cooper, Lou Reed), Queen and Jobriath

9 The descending major chords of 'Changes', 'All the Young Dudes', 'Tumbling Down' and many other glam classics

10 The self-rebirth implicit in glam names: e.g. Marc Bolan, David Bowie, Gary Glitter, Johnny Thunders, Alvin Stardust. Best-ever glam monicker? Ariel Bender

glam!

in: strange changes

'There's a new sensation, a fabulous creation . . .'
                                          Roxy Music

Andrew Logan, *19* magazine, 1974

Early in 1971, amidst a morass of novelty schlock and formulaic bubblegum, a siren sound began floating over the airwaves, wafting from the brickies' transistor radios one passed on the frosty trudge to school.

In essence the song was nothing more than a twelve-bar blues, but it had little to do with the crude grit of Chicago's South Side, or even with the earnest twiddling of the British blues boom. It was a pop blues delivered with mincing swishiness, in a cheek-suckingly camp voice flanked on its fruity 'la la la' fade-out by a pair of wailing falsetto clowns called Flo and Eddie. It was called 'Hot Love', and it was by T. Rex.

'She ain't no witch and I love the way she twitch, uh huh huh . . .'

Had I not been waking up to pop music at that very moment, I would have known that T. Rex had had a tyrannosaurus-sized hit (No. 2) with 'Ride a White Swan' the previous autumn. But I didn't know. I didn't know that pop was anything except Edison Lighthouse and 'Gimme Dat Ding'. (Sure, my parents had a few Beatles forty-fives knocking around the house, but the Beatles were over and their records part of a vanished world called the sixties.) I didn't know and I wasn't terribly interested.

Hearing Marc Bolan for the first time – before I ever knew what he looked like, before I could see that he *weren't no square with his corkscrew hair* – was my password to the mystery of pop's power and glamour. His was the tacky tune that seduced me and kept me coming back for more and more and more, until almost all I had left were the memories of that primal pop thrill.

Imagine, then, how it felt to see Bolan on telly for the first time – to see him just a few months later, sibilating into the microphone as he sang the words to 'Get It On' on *Top of the Pops*, his corkscrew curls bouncing around his tiny elfin countenance. As a vision of pure pop androgyny in glitter and satin pants it was never to be topped. I was transfixed, mesmerized by this puckish punk pixie, part tart and part mystic Pied Piper. Was he a boy or a girl? Would he come on to me or would he lead me to cosmic enlightenment?

Actually, all I could really think was, Please, God, don't let my mother walk into the room right now . . .

*

What an amazing thing to enter the choppy straits of puberty with the glam rock of Bolan and Bowie and Roxy Music as the party tape you carried around in your head. What a fabulous way to become a pop fantasist! At night I'd lie awake with my tiny tranny tuned to Radio Luxembourg, drifting into sleep with images of Marc and his orange Les Paul flashing across the screen in my mind. (All my memories of the period are somehow bound up with guitars, or with forty-five r.p.m. record labels: the EMI red and purple of 'Telegram Sam', the RCA tangerine of 'Starman', the Polydor red of 'Mama Weer All Crazee Now'.)

Glam – or glitter, or whatever you want to call it[1] – arrived at a point when pop was screaming for a new musical wave, a teenage rampage to rival the one with which our older brothers and sisters and cousins had been blessed in that vanished swinging world. Glam was a reaction – exploding, plastic, inevitable – both to the pompous 'progressive' rock to which those older siblings were now in thrall and to the banal bubblegum with which teenagers had had to make do in the era of flared denims and free festivals. (Bowie's 'All the Young Dudes', the national anthem of glam, made this explicit: *'And my brother's back at home/With his Beatles and his Stones/We never got it off on that revolution stuff/What a drag, too many snags'.*[2])

'You'd had this so-called blues boom in England in the sixties, and people looked pretty denim-y and uninteresting,' recalled B. P. Fallon, T. Rex's publicist. 'There was too much grey. What was needed after that was something flash and loud and vulgar and, to some people, annoying. Marc was very shiny. He brought that in, and it actually opened the door for Bowie. Suddenly men were checking their eye make-up. And the music was much more forthright and jumping,

1 Americans tended to call it glitter rock, principally because of Gary Glitter. In the US, the term 'glam' became more current with the rise of the 'big hair' metal bands in the eighties – of which more in the final chapter.
2 When *Rolling Stone* arranged a meeting between Bowie and William Burroughs in November 1973, Bowie said that 'people who are into groups like Alice Cooper, the New York Dolls and Iggy Pop' were 'denying totally and irrevocably the existence of people who are into the Stones and the Beatles'. Pop's generation gap, he argued, had 'decreased from twenty years to ten years'.

much more below the belt. [Marc] created his own image. He wanted adulation and he didn't pretend that he didn't want it. Up until then it wasn't cool to let on that you wanted people to scream at you. People didn't scream at Jethro Tull.'

'The pop scene is *always* waiting for an explosion,' says Laurence Myers, whose Gem Toby Organization was the umbrella management company for both David Bowie and Gary Glitter. 'In the mid-sixties, there was the breakthrough of bands writing their own music and becoming self-contained: that was *the* enormous breakthrough. And then the early seventies was the era of the producer and the songwriter again, so I chose to manage producers and songwriters. Really we would all have been terribly happy if we could have continued making Edison Lighthouse and "Winchester Cathedral" records, because there was no aggravation. But then along came the Bowies, and people like me became the bridge between the industry and the maverick artists. We were able to deal with the tantrums but we could also understand the problems of running an enormous record company.'

The genius of glam was that it was all *about* stardom. It said flaunt it if you've got it, and if you haven't got it fake it – make it up with make-up, cover your face with stardust, reinvent yourself as a Martian androgyne. Glam was prefab, anti-craft, allied to artifice and the trash aesthetic. Its plasticity and cartoonish bisexuality were all about giving pop back to 'the kids', yanking it from the hands of droopy acoustic introverts and pompous Marshall-stacked overlords. It was simple, flash, throwaway, and from 1970 till 1974 it injected more fun into the pop-culture bloodstream than people knew what to do with. Even when the bubblegum boys moved in and served up Gary Glitter and Suzi Quatro, the music and the images were preposterously entertaining.

Glam swept the nation in ways that were at once innocent and morally subversive. It called into question received notions of truth and authenticity, especially in the area of sexuality. It blurred the divide between straights and queers, inviting boys and girls to experiment with images and roles in a genderless utopia of eyeliner and seven-inch platform boots. And it flirted openly with a decadence pitched somewhere between *Cabaret* and *A Clockwork Orange* (into which I was sneaked as a twelve-year-old by the rather roguish father of a schoolchum). Through David Bowie's patronage, the larger pop world was introduced to those *éminences grises* Lou Reed and Iggy Pop, both of them more credible chroniclers of transgression and perversion than the more opportunistic Alice Cooper.

'By whatever mysterious underground channels the decadent sensibility has been conveyed from nineteenth-century Paris and London to twentieth-century New York,' the prurient Albert Goldman could write in 1974, 'the fact is that we are living unconsciously, inadvertently, rather casually, the dread, degenerate, opium-dream existence fantasized by radical writers a hundred years ago. Everybody's walking around in crushed velvet and Parisian brothel boots. People's faces are painted up like Toulouse-Lautrec *demi-mondaines*. They're as languorous as dandies, as jaded as aesthetes, as narcoleptic as absinthe drinkers.' Goldman was half right, but there was a world of difference between Lou Reed's 'Walk on the Wild Side' and the Sweet's 'Ballroom Blitz'.

There were those who dismissed glam as frivolous, narcissistic, politically evasive. Dick Hebdidge in *Subculture: The Meaning of Style* (1979) saw Bowie, Roxy and Lou Reed as artists whose 'extreme foppishness, incipient élitism and morbid pretensions to art and intellect effectively precluded the growth of a larger mass audience'. (Just how much larger a 'mass audience' did he think Bowie should have had?) Hebdidge even quoted a pair of dour Marxist sociologists to support his contention that 'Bowie has in effect colluded in consumer capitalism's attempt to create a dependent adolescent class, involved as passive teenage consumers in the purchase of leisure . . .' instead of questioning 'the value and meaning of adolescence'. Quite apart from the absurd picture this presents – *"Ere, d'yer wanna come round mine and question the value and meaning of adolescence?'* – it's extraordinary to suggest that glam fans, of all teenage subcultures, weren't actively challenging the gender types and work-ethic puritanism of Little England.

In some ways, though, Hebdidge's complaints tally with the way the seventies have been depicted in the movies and memoirs of the present decade – as a fount of kitsch and hedonism, of bad taste and conspicuous waste, rather than as a period of complexity and progressiveness. And while no one is suggesting that we take Suzi Quatro too seriously, the sociological ramifications of glam rock were too far-reaching to be dismissed so lightly. Through glam a generation of sexual misfits was able to accept itself and make its voice heard in the decades to come. Through glam, punk came into being and overthrew the sated rock élite. Rooted in glam, the most interesting artists of the eighties – from Soft Cell to the Pet Shop Boys – saved that decade from becoming one long vapid promo video.

'When it came right down to it,' reminisced Charles Shaar Murray in a 1977 reappraisal of the period, 'glitter carried with it the seeds of its own destruction, but that's OK too. It was the first real *pop* thing that happened in the seventies and it brought a great cast with it, a cast of geniuses and madmen, poseurs and philosophers, winners and losers, clowns and warriors, stars and fools.'

'In a way, I always thought the glam part was the wrong idea to focus on,' says Brian Eno, one of the era's most whimsical stars. 'For me it wasn't about glamour so much as the idea of changing identity or thinking up your own identity. Whether it was glamorous or not was actually accidental.'

Twenty years after glam had withered on the pop vine, Eno sat watching the outrageous Minty perform at the annual Alternative Miss World show – a glam fixture ever since its inception in the early seventies. 'It made me genuinely glad to be English, to see that much bizarreness and wit and kinkiness and inter-gender flirting,' he noted in the diary that became *A Year with Swollen Appendices* (1996).

Not too much had changed since Eno was mincing around in drag as the deranged synthesizer player with Roxy Music.

the prettiest stars

'Girls will be boys and boys will be girls/it's a mixed-up, mumbled-up, shook-up world . . .'

The Kinks

Mickey Finn and Marc Bolan: T. Rex, 1971

London, January 1970. A new pop decade has begun, and two of its budding stars are huddled together at the Trident recording studio, down in old Soho. David Bowie, whose session this is, is coming off the back of a big novelty pop hit, 'Space Oddity', while his friend Marc

Bolan – busy adding some lead guitar licks to his friend's song 'The Prettiest Star' – is about to release the final Tyrannosaurus Rex album, *A Beard of Stars*.

The two men have known each other for two years – they may even have had a fleeting affair of the kind that was only too common in the London pop scene of the sixties. Both have emerged from the dandyish mod scene of the early sixties before adapting to the more folky, flowery style of the decade's second half. Both are hungry for fame.

'Marc was thrilled that someone wanted to use him as a session musician,' says Tony Visconti, who produced the track. 'He was dying to prove that he could *play*. So he came in with his little amp, and he'd learned the song and practised really hard. And David was really chuffed, because he loved Marc – he was probably more in love with Marc than Marc was in love with him. So Marc did his solo and everyone applauded. Suddenly Marc's wife, June, turned viciously on David and said, "We're gonna go now – Marc is too good to play on your record!" And I was stunned. It was the first time I realized there was any rivalry between them.'[1]

Two years later, Britain will be in the frenzied grip of T. Rexstasy and Ziggymania – of glam rock – and the 'friendly rivalry' between Bolan and Bowie will reach fever pitch.

One could argue, of course, that glam began with Elvis Presley, a Dixie Adonis who wore gold suits and caked his eyes with mascara. Or at least with Little Richard, campest of all rock's founding fathers. 'Glamour' was an intrinsic part of pop from its inception, and took a back seat only when boys next door like the Beatles chose to dress down and dissolve the visual barrier between themselves and their hysterical, panty-wetting fans. (The word 'glamour' is of Scottish ori-

[1] 'This was the only time they could have played together,' Visconti told author Dave Thompson in 1987. '[It was] the only time their egos would have allowed it.' The story that Bowie was one of several people handclapping on T. Rex's 1968 hit 'Debora' is pure apocrypha. 'It's hearsay, it's what fans would love to believe,' says Visconti. 'If David Bowie had appeared on any of his records, believe me, Marc would have been the first to talk about it.' Nor was Bowie present on any of the later T. Rex albums, contrary to several accounts.

gin, signifying a kind of 'haze in the air' around people and objects.)

But dandyism of the self-conscious kind that glam would formalize had roots that went back still further: to the foppery of the Restoration and of Beau Brummell, to the obsessive aestheticism of Huysmans's *A rebours* and Wilde's *Picture of Dorian Gray*, to the silent-screen androgyny of Garbo and Valentino. Dandyism as a way of life, as a decadent mode of being running counter to everything deemed 'natural', was destined to feed into pop culture, if only because the little girls who understood seemed to prefer their heart-throbs effeminate. In her *Sexual Personae*, Camille Paglia saw the degenerate dandyism of Baudelaire and his contemporaries as a repudiation of Rousseauist back-to-nature ideals; in the same way, the effeminacy and androgyny of glam rock overturned the scruffy heterosexuality of the Woodstock generation.[2]

'The androgynous is certainly one of the great images of camp sensibility,' wrote Susan Sontag in her celebrated 'Notes on Camp' (1964). 'Examples: the swooning, slim, sinuous figures of Pre-Raphaelite painting and poetry; the thin, flowing, sexless bodies in Art Nouveau prints and bodies . . . the haunting androgynous vacancy behind the perfect beauty of Greta Garbo.' What is most beautiful in

---

2 'Dandyism borders on the spiritual and the stoical,' wrote Baudelaire. It is, he said, 'a kind of religion', albeit a 'weird' one which recognizes 'a grandeur in all follies, an energy in all excess'. Unlike his British predecessor Beau Brummell, who sought to escape his middle-class roots via a subversion of the traditional form of aristocracy, Baudelaire lived in an age of aristocratic decline. Thus he 'did not set himself above, but below the bourgeoisie', aestheticizing the role in which society placed him and fulfilling Camille Paglia's first principle of decadent art: the (re)creation of the self as a 'manufactured object', or the 'product of biology manipulated for art'. This subversive use of civilizing, ordering power against civilization is deemed by Paglia to be a 'daemonization of the Apollonian'. To become 'unnatural', then, is to become exceptional, singular, allowing the dandy to supplant God as creator. The dandy-self is a kaleidoscopic image-machine, continually producing an array of singular, spectacular and even deliberately shocking personae. (Baudelaire at one time sported 'a head of hair freshly dyed green', exulting in both 'the joy of astonishing others' and 'the proud satisfaction of never oneself being shocked'.) My thanks to John Walker, from whose unpublished dissertation 'Framing Dionysus: The Gutter-Dandy in Western Culture' these ideas are extracted.

virile men, Sontag remarked, is 'something feminine (and vice versa)'.

Had Sontag been writing three years later, she could have added to her list a whole flotilla of epicene pop stars. Were there any more dandyish creatures in the firmament of sixties pop than those heterosexual guitar gods Jimi Hendrix and Eric Clapton? (Hendrix had once been scolded by Little Richard for wearing a ruffled shirt on stage: *I'm the only one allowed to dress pretty*,' quoth he of the towering pompadour.) How about the delicately fey Syd Barrett, all lace cuffs and frilly silk shirts, or the group that did more than anybody to disseminate effeminacy in pop, the Rolling Stones?

If Mick Jagger and Brian Jones used camp principally to underscore their basic machismo[3] – when the Stones dressed in drag for their 'Have You Seen Your Mother, Baby, Standing in the Shadow' promo film, they were merely ridiculing female stereotypes – they none the less created a climate in which boys could flirt with homosexuality as a mode, a pose. Jagger's wiry androgyny was a potent rejection of 'straight' masculinity, heavily inspired by the foppish bisexual aristocrats with whom the Stones were consorting. 'In London in the late sixties there was a great honouring of the homosexual side of life,' wrote Marianne Faithfull in her autobiography, *Faithfull*. 'It didn't express itself overtly, it was just in the air everywhere.'

'Coming to London was pure culture shock,' says the Brooklyn-born Tony Visconti. 'I was actually seeing people walking around the streets of London looking like Austin Powers, in crushed velvet jackets and high Edwardian collars. The first time I met Brian Jones was at a Procol Harum session, and Procol Harum still looked like your average poor rock musicians. Brian walked in with French lace cuffs on his shirtsleeves and ruffled lace spilling over and jewellery – he looked like someone from a French court! I thought, Wow, these people actually *dress* like this! I mean, no men wore make-up in America apart from drag queens. Anything gay in New York was *very* covert.

3 In his text for David Bailey's *Pin-Ups*, Francis Wyndham wrote that although Mick Jagger's outline suggested Aubrey Beardsley, his image was one of 'nervous virility rather than epicene languor'. On the other hand, Anita Pallenberg has claimed – in an interview in David Dalton's *The Rolling Stones: The First Twenty Years* – that Jagger and Jones actually had 'a fling'.

So I realized after a few days that this wasn't Kansas any more, Toto.'

Such was the impact of the Stones' demonic dandyism that even a Southern American country boy like Gram Parsons could be found camping it up in the Los Angeles of the late sixties. 'Painted nails, all that effeminate shit,' grunted Flying Burrito Brothers roadie Jimmie Seiter to Parsons biographer Ben Fong-Torres. 'He'd come out of the house holding hands with Keith [Richards], skipping along. He'd come to the Palomino when it was a real truck-driver place, in these faggy outfits, and the other guys [in the Burritos] would say, "We can't go on stage with this fucker."'[4]

'We *all* got faggier by the day,' maintained Stones chronicler Stanley Booth, who like Parsons hailed from the deeply non-androgynous swamp town of Waycross, Georgia. 'The wonder is that by the end of the [1969 Stones] tour we weren't all wearing *dresses*. We all had to brush our hair out of our eyes every eight seconds. You never saw a more limp-wristed bunch of sissies.'

It's interesting to learn that David Bailey wanted to cast Mick Jagger in a pre-Kubrick movie version of *A Clockwork Orange*, and that Anthony Burgess's novel exerted a powerful hold over the mind of the Stones' bisexual, mascara-wearing manager Andrew Loog Oldham. Both Jagger and Burgess's anti-hero Alex were key prototypes for the sexually ambiguous stars of glam rock.[5] 'If this vision of the hoodlum as poet is a vastly influential falsehood based essentially on the homosexual temperament,' wrote J. Marks-Highwater, one of Jagger's more eccentric biographers, 'the importance of homosexuality to pop culture is also quite undeniable. Camp, put-ons and a special kind of grotesque self-mockery are indispensable elements of pop's basic sensibility.'

Actually, it's surprising that there wasn't a great deal *more* androgyny

4 In a piece for the *LA Weekly*, Miss Mercy of legendary groupie ensemble the GTOs recalled her first sight of Parsons thus: 'The lights dimmed and a tall lean cat in a sparkling Nudie suit drifted by. He was true glitter, true glamour rock. The suit sparkled like diamonds; it had submarines all over it outlined in rhinestones and the color was scarlet red . . .'

5 According to photographer Mick Rock, David Bowie too was always talking about *A Clockwork Orange*. Many of Bowie's 1972 shows began with Walter Carlos's electronic version of Beethoven's 'Ode to Joy' from the film soundtrack.

in pop at the turn of the decade. Even the Stones seemed to have toned things down somewhat at this point in their career. Ray Davies may have sounded a bold note with the transvestism of 'Lola', but around him lay a barren land of bearded denim noodlers. After the psychedelic overload of 1967 and the street violence of 1968, rock seemed to retreat from its flamboyant messianism. The years 1969 and 1970 were all about getting it together in the country, rejecting stardom. 'The make-up and all that wasn't a brand-new idea,' recalled Mick Ronson before his death in 1993. 'But it had gone. Everybody was into looking authentic.'

Was pop ever cursed by a more specious concept than 'authenticity'? As Simon Frith put it in 1973 (apropos of Bowie's supposed 'selling out'), 'Where is this authentic rock tradition, pose-less and glamour-free? Elvis? The Beatles? No way. Dylan wasn't a bootlace-maker, pulling himself up. They're all pop stars, big business, livery-chauffeured.' (One of the most enduring images from this period in pop was Guy Peellaert's study of Bob Dylan, an enigmatic god in shades and fur, cocooned in a limousine, in *Rock Dreams*. Like many of the images in that remarkable collection – including those of the Stones, Bowie and Bolan – it defined, and possibly even helped to shape, the macabre decadence of the early seventies. Peellaert would go on to design the covers of Bowie's *Diamond Dogs* and the Stones' *It's Only Rock 'n' Roll*.)

With the beginning of the new decade, the tide turned again. The seeds had already been planted with the birth of Gay Liberation after the Stonewall riots in New York, and of the glitter-punk monsters that were Iggy Pop and Alice Cooper. Tiring of the Woodstock Nation's stoned platitudes, a new breed of misfit was starting to revolt. 'Brian [Slade] despised the hypocrisy of the peace and love generation,' remarks gay manager Cecil Drake in Todd Haynes's film *Velvet Goldmine*. '[He] felt his music spoke far more to its orphans and its outcasts. *His* revolution, he used to say, will be a sexual one.'

In Britain, the most pointed and violent reaction to hippiedom took the form of the skinheads, who shaved their hair, sneered at rock, and danced to soul and reggae records. In part this reflected a class schism, but then Britain's class system had always had more to do with style and tribalization than its American counterpart. Skins were against everything wimpy and long-haired and middle class, which is what rock had become by the end of the sixties. With their football hooliganism and brutal appearance – the Crombie overcoats, bleached jeans and eight-eyed Doc Martens – the skinheads were the ultimate bogeyboys of British culture at the turn of the decade. What set them apart from earlier tribes like rockers and mods was their utter lack of interest in particular pop stars: forerunners of disco culture, they were music consumers whose real stars were turntables. Even when the pre-glam Slade gave themselves a Ben-Sherman-shirts-and-braces makeover, skinheads paid them little attention.

The skins may not have affected the course of white pop, but they were symptomatic of a desire for teenage change in an ossifying world. Like them, Marc Bolan was tuned in to pop's post-Woodstock mood. As early as the summer of 1969, indeed, Bolan was prepared to alienate hardcore fans of his fey hippie duo T. Rex by recording the electric pop single 'King of the Rumbling Spires'. 'It doesn't actually sound that much different, just more funky,' he said at the time. 'We always played pop music anyway, and to me it's completely fair to use electricity.'

It was hardly as though Bolan was unacquainted with electric pop. He'd trashed guitars à la Pete Townshend in the mod band John's Children in the sixties, and had at least one eye fixed on pop stardom from his earliest days as a cherubic mod model. 'Marc was a wonderful fraud,' recalled John's Children manager – and Bolan bedmate – Simon Napier-Bell. 'His guitar playing was unbelievably bad, but I just loved that voice. I thought he'd be the biggest star in the world.' For Bolan, the Tolkien-inspired songs about elves and unicorns were simply a stylistic diversion, a tailoring of his music to fit the times. Bolan's sub-Donovan, hippie-changeling persona – he would perform sitting cross-legged on stage while Steve 'Peregrine' Took tapped a set of bongos beside him – nearly paid off with the divine 'Debora' (1968), but when the time came to move on he happily ignored the dissenting underground voices. Two years later, with Took replaced by the gorgeous Mickey Finn, *A Beard of Stars* was released as the first fully electric album by Tyrannosaurus Rex.

'There was a track called "Elemental Child", an instrumental at the end of side two, and Marc played electric guitar on it,' says David Enthoven, then managing T. Rex. 'We focused in on that, we thought it was fantastic, and you can't really play electric guitar sitting down. We talked to Marc about doing something different, about standing up, and he had Mickey Finn in with him. The idea was just to get a band together. There wasn't any great science behind it, except for the fact that Marc started to play electric guitar.'

'There was nothing extraordinary in his shift at all,' said John Peel, the underground DJ who'd been an avid champion of T. Rex. 'He was just a quite ambitious lad with a small gift and a lot of good reference points who enjoyed being mildly famous. By 1970, '71, people had realized that the counterculture was a bit of a joke.'

'I was very unhappy with the way we were really being ignored by the media of all sorts and the papers and the radio and that,' Bolan told Michael Wale in 1971. 'I'd hear something like a new Dylan record or a new Beatles record or a Who record and I'd know that I was as funky as them, you know, it wasn't an ego number. And I knew I was on that sort of level of being an artist – I felt I should be reaching people.' The cockney princeling decided it was hitsville or bust. In August 1970 – egged on by his wife – he set about writing a song that would *have* to crack the Top Ten.

The result was 'Ride a White Swan', in Bolan's words 'a two-minute thirty-second, funky, snappy foot-tapper' that brilliantly combined kiddie-singalong cadences with an electric neo-rockabilly groove. '*Ride it all out like a bird in the skyways/Ride it all out like-a you were a bird,*' he warbled over the kind of crunchy Les Paul riff that would define all the great Bolan singles. It sounded like Donovan wedded to Chuck Berry, and it spelled T. Rex.

When 'White Swan' climbed to No. 2 on the charts, it was too much for the heads who'd grocked on cross-legged Marc at the Middle Earth in Covent Garden. This was a Judas act akin to Dylan's apostasy on the electric 1966 tour, and Bolan was never forgiven for it. 'I see no reason why freaks shouldn't be on the charts, but then they turn around and resent you for it,' he sighed to Pete Frame. 'I'm probably more ethnic now than I ever was, much more, because I'm more involved in the art of producing good funky energy rock music.'

'*Fly it all out like a needle in a sunbeam/Fly it all out like-a you were a bird . . .*'

If Marc pretended that he saw no clear division between rock and pop, he couldn't argue with the obvious fact that it was downy-faced teenagers who were buying 'White Swan'. 'I couldn't believe it the first time I went out on stage and saw all those little white faces,' he said. 'No one is going to convince me that their enthusiasm is a bad thing for Rex. If there is going to be any revolution in pop, it must come from the young people, and if you ignore them you are cutting yourself off from the life supply of the rock music force.'

'There was a kind of gap in the market,' recalled Nina Myskow, former editor of pubescent female bible *Jackie*. 'We hadn't got our own Osmonds or Jackson Five, and yet the whole Beatles era was obviously over. Everyone was just waiting for something like T. Rex to happen.' *Jackie* leapt into the breach by printing full-colour posters of the pouting, curly-locked Bolan. *Top of the Pops*, meanwhile, rejoiced that it had found a star who was as telegenic as he was musically titillating. 'You have to remember that *Top of the Pops* was *everything* then, *everything*,' says Nicky Chinn. 'Today it doesn't sell a copy, but then it really sold records.'

By early 1971 T. Rex had been retooled as a full electric quartet and Bolan's lyrics stripped of references to diamond meadows and seagull women. Suddenly the imagery was flip, futuristic, strewn with sci-fi vixens and sexy American cars. It was urban pop art. 'I've got this sound in my head that is definitely unlike anything else we've put out,' Bolan claimed. 'It really is cosmic rock. I'd like to catch on the record the essence of the audiences we're getting so that people will know what is happening. People who've come to the gigs cannot believe it. It really is like the old rock days.' With Steve Currie on bass, Bill Legend on drums and Flo and Eddie on shriekingly camp backing vocals, the group got pie-eyed on brandy one night and cut 'Hot Love' at four in the morning. 'It was done as a happy record, and I wanted to make a twelve-bar record a hit, which hasn't been done since "Hi Heel Sneakers" really.' In late February the song became T. Rex's first No. 1 hit.

'The T. Rex sound was pure kismet,' says Tony Visconti. 'It was a story about how the right people met each other at the right time. Bill Legend and Steve Currie are never given the credit they were due. Bill was a unique drummer, from the Ringo Starr school. Steve Currie came from a jazz background, which explains a lot of his choice of notes that weren't typical rock notes. Marc was not a classic electric guitarist, he didn't come up through the Eric Clapton or Jimmy Page schools. It was more as if the Hobbit had learned how to play electric guitar! So here was a band of musicians who technically shouldn't have sounded good together, but it was like winning the pools – Marc picked the right numbers and got himself a killer team.

'The other secret is that the records were made very quickly. Because of Marc's own economic restrictions – he thought it was wrong to squander money on studio time – we recorded very fast. No T. Rex album took more than three and a half weeks, four weeks, to produce, if you totalled the time. The recordings don't sound perfect, but boy do they sound fresh. The vibe is so incredible because everyone is so hopped up, playing with great spirit, playing by the seat of their pants because they'd only just learned the songs. The trick was: Follow Marc, make him look good.'

Almost as significant as T. Rex's chart success was Bolan's new get-up, particularly the women's clothes he was buying in the World's End. 'June employed Tony Secunda's wife, Chelita, as T. Rex's publicist, and Chelita saw that Marc was very pretty,' says Visconti. 'It was her idea to take Marc around town and hit the women's shops, getting him the feather boas and the beautifully embroidered jackets he wore. There was a place in the World's End that sold clothes which were considered kind of kitsch. That famous chartreuse satin jacket with the music notes embroidered on it – this was pure kitsch, and musicians weren't really dressing like that yet. Marc took it very seriously and started walking around like that. I don't remember anyone before him wearing those vivid colours.'

Topping it all off was the boldest statement of all – the make-up. With 'Hot Love' at No. 1, Bolan made a spur-of-the-moment decision to let Chelita put glitter under his eyes before appearing on *Top of the Pops*. 'Chelita was the first person to really make up Marc,' says Visconti. 'She didn't just put some eye make-up on him, she threw glitter on his cheeks.' Marc claimed he'd done it purely for a laugh and thought no more about it, but at the next T. Rex gig he was greeted by the sight of hundreds of beglittered fans. For thrill-starved juveniles the length and breadth of Britain, glam was born on that Thursday's *Top of the Pops*.

'As soon as he got seen on TV, basically it all took off,' says David Enthoven. 'Marc definitely started it. He was the first to put glitter on his face, and I think that had a lot to do with his wife. June had the vision about how to present this little pixie. It was definitely a team. She was very instrumental in picking Mickey, who wasn't much of a musician but was fucking great-looking. The contrast between Marc and Mickey was irresistible. To be honest, we didn't go out to target fifteen-year-olds, it was television that did that. It was fairly organic, how it happened; there wasn't any grand plan to start glam rock. All Marc really did was give pop some attitude. He made it glamorous, and he made it different.'

Top: Marc Bolan at the peak of T.Rextasy, 1972

Malcom McDowell in *A Clockwork Orange*, 1971

Left: David Bowie contemplates the face of the future, Beckenham, 1972

Below: Angie Bowie, the power behind Ziggy's throne

'Like a leper messiah': Bowie as Ziggy

Opposite (*left*): Eno and Andy Mackay on an
early Roxy date; (*right*) Bryan Ferry

The cover of *Roxy Music.* 1972

Roxy Music

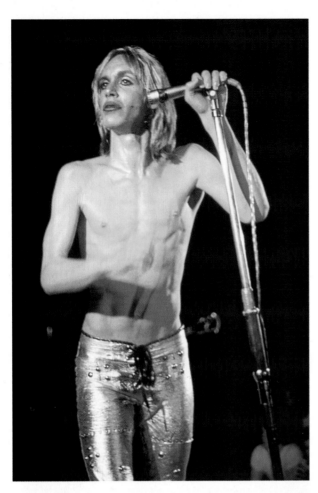

Opposite: Lou Reed in his Freddi Buretti outfit, summer 1972

Left: Iggy Pop at the King's Cross Cinema, June 1972

Lou Reed makes a cameo appearance with Bowie and the Spiders, Royal Festival Hall, July 1972

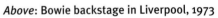

Above: Bowie backstage in Liverpool, 1973

Bowie's footwear

Ziggy girls in Dunstable, summer 1973

gimme danger

'I think rock should be tarted up, made into a prostitute, a parody of itself. It should be the clown, the Pierrot medium.'

David Bowie, April 1971

Bowie in transition, late 1971

Marc Bolan figured he wasn't doing anything so wild by wearing glitter on *Top of the Pops*. 'I don't really care what people think,' he said. 'If the thing works, it works. Elvis Presley wore eye make-up for years. People thought he had dark sultry eyes. Mick Jagger has wonderful skin embellishment. People are really works of art, and if you have a nice face you might as well play about with it. It gets boring otherwise. Two hundred years ago, men covered themselves with something scented or wore powdered wigs and faces. If someone is prudish enough not to realize that it's all been done before, they're very stupid. Anyway, I don't believe chicks like really butch guys – apart from wrestlers. Valentino was living proof of that.'

Paying close attention to Bolan's image rethink was his friend and rival David Bowie – who, let's face it, had never been the butchest of guys. Indeed, the 'Space Oddity' boy had consistently flirted with spangled apparel and cross-dressing, to the extent of actually wearing a dress on the cover of 1970s *The Man Who Sold the World*. For a show in February 1970 supporting Country Joe McDonald at London's Round House, Bowie's kooky bisexual girlfriend Angela kitted him out in a glittery 'Rainbowman' costume, with Mick Ronson dressed as 'Gangsterman', bassist Tony Visconti as 'Hypeman' and drummer John Cambridge as 'Cowboyman'. In front of a patchouli-scented Country Joe audience, the spectacle was greeted with incredulous sniggering.

'It came off as no more than everyone dressing up,' Bowie admitted ruefully in hindsight. 'I was in silver lamé and blue and silver cloak and blue hair and the whole thing, glitter everywhere. The whole thing was on that scale . . . and we died a death. And of course the boys said, "Look, I told you so. Let's get back to just being a band again." That's the period which broke me up. I just about stopped after that performance, because I knew it was right. I knew it was what I wanted to do and I knew it was what people would want eventually.'

Did he? There are more than a few people who thought it was actually Angela – Angie Bowie after the couple's nuptials in March 1970 – who'd upped the showbiz stakes; Angela who was pressing Bowie to don ever more extreme costumes and make-up; Angela who was encouraging him to draw on his experiences as a member, in the sixties, of Lindsay Kemp's notorious Underground Mime Troupe. It was Angie

Bowie who established a kind of pop salon in the couple's home, Haddon Hall in Beckenham, and who dragged her husband along to a gay Kensington discotheque called the Sombrero Club.

'I would say Angela is just as responsible for creating glam rock as David,' says Tony Visconti. 'Angie made David realize how outrageous he could be – he certainly wouldn't have done it without her permission. Angela and my girlfriend, Liz, were the seamstresses, the designers of these clothes we wore at the Round House. And that night is probably when glam rock was born. The audience was mixed: the hippie types were booing us, but some people were fascinated. It was awkward. And as much as David shuns glam rock now, he still would like to take credit for this.'

Crouching to one side of the Round House stage, significantly, was the impish figure of Marc Bolan. Visconti claims Bowie hadn't even been aware of Bolan's presence till he was looking at photographer Ray Stevenson's contact strip with a magnifying glass one night in 1977. 'I would say the Round House gig planted the seed in Marc's head,' Visconti says, 'and that the two men simultaneously kind of invented this.'

What Bowie and Bolan both saw was that 'glamour' was the antithesis of hippiedom: for long-hair puritans, glamour symbolized affluence, capitalism, 'show business'. As late as 1974, the majority of the punters at the Round House – where I regularly saw Sunday afternoon bills composed of pub-rockers and West Coast wannabes – were still aggressively dressing down, muttering curses on 'teeny-bop' music. Bowie's brilliance was to see that he could bridge the gulf between young adult dropouts and hungry teenagers. To the 'heads' in their greatcoats and loon pants, he proved you could dress up and still make great music.

If Angie Bowie had been instrumental in pressing David to do the Round House show, she was no less persuasive when it came to entrusting his career to a man who would lend new meaning to the word hype. Twenty-seven-year-old Tony DeFries was working for the legal firm of Godfrey Davis and Batt when, in April 1970, he was handed the job of working out a settlement between Bowie and Bowie's first manager, Ken Pitt. The son of a Shepherd's Bush antique dealer, DeFries had always been captivated by show business and had represented various models and photographers in the late sixties. Now he saw a real opportunity to make his mark and wasted no time in seizing it.

'Tony DeFries was a very bright man,' says Laurence Myers, to whose Gem Toby Organization DeFries signed Bowie the following year. 'He came to me and said there was an opportunity to become David Bowie's manager. And that's what happened: Bowie was signed to my company and Tony was his designated manager.' Myers himself was an old-school pop businessman, having started out as an accountant working for Mickie Most and Allen Klein. Nothing could quite have prepared him for Bowie and his Haddon Hall entourage.

'I remember that David was very, very impressed with Marc Bolan,' says Myers. 'We were *all* impressed with Bolan, because he was just so different. But I remember saying to David, girls don't buy pop stars who wear dresses, they buy Cliff and Tom Jones and David Cassidy. And he patted me on the head and said, "Don't you worry, Laurence, it'll all be alright," and I wrote another cheque. I would pay bills where there was no instant direct obvious financial benefit, because I always had the feeling that out of it would come something enormous. He just had this very good sense of what he was and the people he wanted to get to.'

One group of people who recognized the significance of Angie Bowie to her husband was the cast of Andy Warhol's *Pork*, who came to London for a run at the Round House in August 1971. Eighteen months on from Bowie's fiasco at the very same venue, with T. Rex's 'Get It On' at the top of the singles chart, the Bowies went to see the scandalous production and wound up befriending its principal performers: the Southern drag queen Wayne County, the bleach-blond scenester Leee Black Childers, the breast-baring Cherry Vanilla and (playing Warhol) the gay actor Tony Zanetta. Yet when the *Pork* people caught a David Bowie gig at the Country Club in Hampstead, they were not impressed. 'Leee and I had already heard of him because we'd read an article in *Rolling Stone*,' wrote Jayne County in her memoir *Man Enough to be a Woman*. 'He'd just released *Hunky Dory*,[1] but the show

---

1 Not true, actually. *Hunky Dory* would not appear till December 1971.

was really disappointing, to be honest. It was a folky act with acoustic guitars and Mick Ronson looking like a dippy hippie.' The *Pork* cast was more taken with Angie, whom County remembered as 'loud, pushy, and fabulous'. 'Of the two Bowies,' remarked Tony Zanetta, 'Angie was definitely the more masculine.'

Bowie was entranced by the *Pork* actors for one simple reason: they were connected with Andy Warhol. (One of the songs he played at the Country Club was his new paean to the platinum-haired artist, the baldly titled 'Andy Warhol'.) Warhol's world had fascinated him ever since Ken Pitt had returned from New York in late 1966 with a copy of the first Velvet Underground album. 'I was the key to Warhol, or something like that,' remembered Zanetta. 'It was a lot about role-playing, and David was lured in the same way . . . he was coming from the same base as we were. Which is basically an inability to be oneself and constructing a new personality in which one could act out one's fantasies and desires.'

Though there were other influences on the creation of his brilliant *alter ego* Ziggy Stardust, the exposure to the no-holds-barred New York sleaze of *Pork* seemed to trigger a new audacity in Bowie. 'You could see it lighting the fuses of all sorts of ideas in his head as he sat there watching those people, every one of them as sharp as you could want a performance artist to be,' wrote Angie Bowie in *Backstage Passes*. For Bowie, the New York scene looked far more decadent and enticing than London's. There was an element of danger there – in the movies of Warhol and the songs of Lou Reed – which was unknown in Britain. New York was about drag queens and junkies, small-town freaks transforming themselves into gutter aristocrats as they revolted against America's repressive homophobia. Warhol had made these people 'superstars', and the Velvets had hymned them in speed-freak anthems like 'Sister Ray'. The Factory was less about radical chic than about hedonist tourism; it was a place where princesses could consort with perverts.

'For David, New York represented the same thing as it did for me,' says the English photographer Mick Rock. 'New York was much more obviously depraved than London, and the self-indulgence was on a level that I had not experienced before, whether it was drugs or wild drag queens. There were people in London like Lindsay Kemp and Andrew Logan who were on the cutting edge, but the Warhol scene was a whole other thing. And Andy could still open up all the doors. To me, Lou represented that dark thing, and David fed off it. Lou was the linchpin, and that's what fascinated David.'

In 1968 the Factory moved from its premises on East 47th Street to a building on the west side of Union Square. The new Factory was within spitting distance of Max's Kansas City, the club on Park Avenue South at 17th Street which now functioned as HQ for Manhattan's decadent *demi-monde*. 'Max's was the exact place where pop art and pop life came together in New York in the sixties,' wrote Warhol in *POPism*. 'Teeny-boppers and sculptors, rock stars and poets from St Mark's Place, Hollywood actors checking out what the underground actors were all about, boutique owners and models, modern dancers and go-go dancers – everybody went to Max's and everything got homogenized there.'

In 1969 the cramped back room at Max's became *the* place to see and be seen, a room where a gawky queen like Wayne County could jab elbows with a celluloid legend like Jane Fonda, or where aspiring unknowns like Patti Smith and Robert Mapplethorpe would wait to be invited in by music-biz players like Elektra's Danny Fields. ('You had to be able to endure a certain amount of humiliation and isolation, because no one would talk to you,' recalled Smith.) Eventually, Max's owner Mickey Ruskin began booking bands for the club's tiny upstairs room: the Velvet Underground's *Live at Max's Kansas City* was recorded there in 1970.

Connected to the Warhol/Max's scene was the underground theatre world, which employed many of the characters who existed on the periphery of the Factory – people like Tony Ingrassia, who had pieced together the Warhol conversations that made up *Pork*. Both Charles Ludlam's Ridiculous Theatrical Company and John Vaccaro's Playhouse of the Ridiculous Theater used street people in their outrageous, viciously satirical productions, which were often written by such Warhol acolytes as Jackie Curtis and Ronnie Tavel. 'The Ridiculous Theater started out with John Vaccaro and Charles Ludlam, and then there was a schism in 1966 or 1967,' says David Johansen, who took some of the Ridiculous ideas with him into the New York Dolls. 'Charles Ludlam created the Ridiculous Theatrical Company and brought some people with him. He was a bona fide genius, his mind was totally unbelievable. He had an incredible grasp of all the great literature and would transform it into really funny plays. There was something awesome about the way he could transform things into high camp.'

Prominent in this theatre, significantly, was the use of glitter as a statement of excess. 'I thought so much of the glam or glitter thing came from Warhol and the Theater of the Ridiculous,' says Lou Reed. 'Jackie Curtis, Holly Woodlawn . . . just the outfits that these people were wearing and the kind of theatre that was going on. The way they were making costumes out of things they found in the street, the use of make-up, men wearing nail polish . . .'

'People had been wearing glitter for a long time and the drag queens were wearing it on the street,' said Leee Black Childers. 'But I think "glitter" really took off when John Vaccaro went shopping for costume material and came across this little place in Chinatown that was having a big clearance sale on their glitter. And he bought it all – giant shopping-bag-size bags of glitter in all colours. Baby Betty, who was playing a thalidomide baby, had glitter coming out of her pussy – so it was because of John Vaccaro that glitter became synonymous with outrageousness.'

Vaccaro himself saw glitter in purely anarchic, subversive terms. 'I never thought of anything as "the glitter movement",' he said. 'I'd been using glitter in theatre since the mid-fifties. But I really wasn't interested in campy things. I wasn't interested in promoting homosexuality. My sensibility is different than camp. There were two schools: the homosexuals and the theatre people. Mine had social content, the others didn't. And I used glitter as a way of presentation. Nothing more. Glitter was the gaudiness of America, that's what I interpreted it as. I used it because it was shoving America back into the American faces. It was the gaudiness of Times Square. You know, take away the lights and what do you have in Times Square? Nothing.'

From the speed-freak trannies of the East Village to the alien pop deity that was Ziggy Stardust, via the Round House production of *Pork*: here is one of the major trunk roads of glam.

'I think Jayne County groomed David,' says Bebe Buell, a permanent fixture on the Max's scene. 'I don't think Jayne and Leee Black Childers are given proper credit for their input, because they really did teach him all about drag queens and transvestites. He didn't know anything about that. He was a little folky before those weirdos got their hands on him. Nor is Angela given enough credit. But people are always embarrassed by where they really got their inspiration.'

'Of course we influenced David to change his image,' said County, who by the autumn of 1971 was spinning Alice Cooper and Mott the Hoople albums in his capacity as the DJ at Max's. 'I'd gotten the shaven eyebrows thing from Jackie Curtis, and David started shaving his eyebrows and painting his nails.' The influence would be consolidated when Tony DeFries made the extraordinary decision to hire the *Pork* freaks to run the American arm of his new MainMan management company. 'Tony DeFries hired Cherry Vanilla, Leee Childers, Tony Zanetta, Jamie DeCarlo,' said County. 'They had all these freaky people around, trying to make David look good. If it hadn't been for *Pork*, there would never have been a MainMan, or for that matter a Ziggy Stardust.'

'What happened was that Tony and David wanted to go and live in America,' says Laurence Myers. 'Tony wanted to open a GTO office in America and manage all the artists in America, but I knew I would lose a fortune if I let him do that. While I was able to be relatively free with money when I knew what was going on, I would not have felt the same if these lunatics had been allowed to run an American office on my chequebook. I told Tony I would fund the opening of MainMan, and that I wanted an override, with a share of the management income and the record income.'

In September 1971 Bowie and DeFries flew to New York to complete his signing to RCA, whose Dennis Katz had just signed Lou Reed to the label. That very night, Katz arranged for Bowie to meet the ex-Velvets frontman at a restaurant called the Ginger Man. Surrounded by A&R men, and with journalist Lisa Robinson breaking the ice, Bowie paid court to Reed and told him that his new song, 'Queen Bitch', was a homage to the Velvets. (On the sleeve of *Hunky Dory*, the words 'Some V.U. White Light Returned with Thanks' are scrawled next to the track's listing.) 'David was flirtatious and coy,' Tony Zanetta told Victor Bockris. 'He was in his Lauren Bacall phase, with his Veronica Lake hairdo and eyeshadow. So he let Lou take the driver's seat conversationally.' Reed, bloated with drink and married to a woman he scorned, let Bowie off lightly, perhaps sensing that this effete creature might be a passport to the revival of his own career.

After dinner the party repaired, inevitably, to Max's Kansas City. Here, with a little assistance from Lisa Robinson and Danny Fields, Bowie was introduced to another of his American heroes, the notorious Iggy Pop. Like the Velvets, Pop's band the Stooges was the antithesis of sixties utopianism. Their first, self-titled album was a sheer negation of that decade's good vibrations: *'Well, it's 1969 OK/All across the USA/It's another year for me and you/Another year with nothin' to do . . .'* As a performer, Iggy was the most unhinged maniac ever to prowl a stage; out of his skull on acid, coke and opiates, he pushed himself to the very edge of self-annihilation. If Reed was cold, clinically nihilistic – a daemonized Apollo, in Camille Paglia's formulation – then Iggy was Dionysus on heroin.

For Bowie, Pop was the genuine article – the id to his ego. Iggy took the abjection of Warhol's superstars to a cartoon extreme. He was a freak, a rock geek, and his attitude was 'punk' years before its time. Naturally, the Max's crowd lapped him up: when Leee Black Childers saw the Stooges at Ungano's in 1970, the performance struck him as 'so sexual, so outrageous, so *unallowed!*' More recently, playing the Electric Circus in June 1971, Iggy had embraced the glam aesthetic by covering himself in glitter and gold and silver spray-paint. This wasn't the Gothic circus of Alice Cooper, it was 'ridiculous theatre', anarchic street transgression. 'Alice Cooper was theatrical, he had all the accoutrements,' recalled Alan Vega of the minimalist electro duo Suicide. 'But with Iggy this was not acting. It was the real thing.'

Bowie, too, saw Iggy's as a 'natural' theatre. 'It's very interesting, because it doesn't conform to any standards or rules or structures of theatre,' he observed. 'It's his own and it's just a Detroit theatre that he's brought with him. It's straight from the street.' Bowie claims that 'nothing of import' was said at Max's that night, but the next morning he and DeFries met with Iggy to discuss working together. 'I think

Bowie's infatuation with Iggy had to do with Bowie wanting to tap into the rock 'n' roll reality that Iggy lived,' said Leee Black Childers. 'And that Bowie could never live because he was a wimpy little south London art student and Iggy was a Detroit trash bag. David Bowie knew he could never achieve the reality that Iggy was born into. So he thought he'd buy it.'

'To give them their due,' Iggy later told Arthur Levy, 'Bowie, DeFries, all the MainMan management people he later hired . . . had a real appreciation for the arts. It went very deep and still does with Bowie. And DeFries is the same way. When I'd talk to DeFries and tell him my ideals and my mad theories about life and theatre and music, he would listen.' For Iggy, DeFries was a larger-than-life huckster, a P. T. Barnum: 'I thought, People will go for this guy. He had a big cigar and a big pointed nose and a great big Afro and a smug look on his face and an English accent and a big fur coat and a belly. And to the people who were running the American industry it just spelled "Hot Manager"!'

'I think glam just gave Iggy an excuse to roll around in glitter and paint himself a different colour,' says Bebe Buell. 'Jim [Jim Osterberg, Iggy's real name] would have done that stuff with or without glitter, just the same as smearing peanut butter over himself or rolling in broken glass. Jim was an original, and none of that stuff had anything to do with fashion.' Lou Reed concurs with this. 'I think Jim likes to rivet an audience with more than just music,' he says. 'He'll use any tool available.'

As if adding Reed and Pop to his trophy cabinet weren't enough, Bowie was granted an audience the next day with Warhol himself. This time the atmosphere was a little frostier, especially after Bowie played him the song 'Andy Warhol'. Desperately sensitive about his appearance, Warhol cringed at the line *Andy Warhol looks a scream*. But the sight of Bowie's yellow patent-leather shoes was enough to win the artist over and the meeting ended cordially.

Back in England, high on the experience of meeting his American mainmen, Bowie plotted his course to glory. By the time *Hunky Dory* was released in December, Ziggy Stardust had been conceived, born and set to music.

'and a queer threw up at the sight of that . . .'

'I could play the wild mutation as a rock and roll star . . .'

David Bowie

Ziggy presents Iggy and Lou: London, June 1972

We will never know exactly what happened in David Bowie's head between September 1971 and January 1972, but we can be sure that it had something to do with his New York experiences. The idea of creating a superstar *alter ego* was an unprecedented brainwave, a strategy of reconstruction that simultaneously parodied and hyperbolized the nature of stardom. To make this *alter ego* a kind of alien hermaphrodite was even more inspired. 'It was one of those instantaneous vision things that you get,' he told Ben Fisher in 1997. 'It all came to me in a daydream about what this thing was all about.'

Almost as unprecedented was the musical quantum leap from *Hunky Dory* to *The Rise and Fall of Ziggy Stardust and the Spiders from Mars*. Steering a midway course between the futuristic blues-metal of *The Man Who Sold the World* and the melodic balladry of *Hunky Dory*, Bowie and Ronson fashioned the perfect seventies pop-rock sound, a sound as plastic and guitar-heavy as T. Rex. It was loud, flashy and apocalyptic: the Velvets and the Stooges filtered through Anthony Newley and Syd Barrett. As a concept album, moreover, it made the Who's *Tommy* sound bombastic.

To give Ziggy the kick-start he deserved, Bowie turned himself into a wild mutation, a polysexual space invader with a carrot-coloured puffball mullet, 'snow-white tan' and skin-tight PVC jumpsuits that only exaggerated his ectomorphic physique. Unlike Iggy Pop (or Mick Ronson, come to that), Ziggy was deliberately unsexy; he wasn't even elfin-cherubic like Bolan. The metamorphosis was a brilliant device: a distancing disguise, a *doppelgänger*. 'By creating Ziggy to go out and front for him,' wrote Angie, 'David never had to act like himself in public if he didn't want to.'

'You wait until you see the stage show,' Bowie told George Tremlett in January. 'It's going to be entertainment. That's what's missing in pop music now – entertainment. There's not much outrageousness left any more, apart from me and Marc Bolan. The Beatles were outrageous at one time and so was Mick Jagger, but you can't remain at the top for five years and still be outrageous . . . you become accepted and the impact has gone.'

Even this wasn't quite enough, and the next day Bowie decided to push the boat still further by announcing to Michael Watts of *Melody Maker* that he was 'gay and always had been'. The fact that it wasn't strictly true – that Bowie had homosexual leanings but was primarily heterosexual – was irrelevant. (Watts himself hinted at the game-playing in his piece: 'There's a sly jollity about how he says it, a secret smile at the corners of his mouth. He knows that in these times it's permissible to act like a male tart, and that to shock and outrage, which pop has always striven to do throughout its history, is a balls-breaking process.')

Six years later, Bowie confessed to the same journalist that he wasn't sure what had prompted the 'confession': 'It certainly wasn't a premeditated thing. I was starting to build Ziggy, he was starting to come together and I was naturally falling into that role. It was using one's own resources and you sort of pick up on bits of your own life when you're putting a role together. Bang! It was suddenly there on the table.'

'Falling into that role': Bowie may not have been gay, but Ziggy Stardust was – and a lot more besides. 'David had to become what Ziggy was, he had to believe in him,' said Mick Ronson. 'Yes, Ziggy affected his personality. But he affected Ziggy's personality. They lived off each other.' Above all, Ziggy enabled Bowie to turn himself into an icon of deviance fit to stand alongside the Lou Reeds and Iggy Pops. 'Ziggy served my purpose,' he recalled, 'because I found it easier to function through him, although I probably put myself on a path of pure psychological damage by doing what I did. But I felt like it was going to be easier living through an alternative self.'

In 1987 Bowie claimed that the birth of Ziggy had been accompanied by 'quite a bit of antagonism': 'Nothing like, say, the Pistols when they got started, but the first couple of months were not easy. The people did find it very hard until we had a musical breakthrough. The actual look and everything, I mean, it was, "Aw, a bunch of poofters", you know? Which was kind of fun. I mean, we played it up a lot. Because it was the most rebellious thing that was happening at the time.'

Tony DeFries was more than happy to exploit the controversy over Bowie's coming out. 'Tony in my view was not a great manager, but I think he did a brilliant job managing Bowie,' says Laurence Myers. 'He realized that Bowie was an immensely talented guy who everybody would want to get to, and he simply put himself between the world and David Bowie. If you wanted to get to Bowie you had to go through Tony DeFries.' By the time 'Starman' was released in April, the hype was paying off. On stage with the Spiders from Mars, Bowie would mime fellatio on the staunchly heterosexual Mick Ronson's guitar, a gimmick that only pointed up Ronson's greater sex appeal to women. With the June release of *Ziggy Stardust* itself, Bowiemania began in earnest. 'The success was very overnight,' said Mick Ronson. 'It was like waking up one morning and finding that we were suddenly superstars, with no preparation for it at all.'

'What DeFries provided for David was a financial security net, and that made a big difference,' says Tony Visconti, whose own distrust of DeFries had led to his parting ways with Bowie. 'With the security that DeFries provided, David made a great album in *Hunky Dory*, and then inventing Ziggy was pure genius. DeFries was the man who provided the machine that would sell anything David wanted to do. If David had wanted to become an ordinary pop star, DeFries would have made *that* possible.'

'MainMan was all rather important in a way,' Bowie admitted. 'I certainly would not have achieved that degree of notoriety without all that nonsense going on . . . Without some of those initial ridiculous fusses, some of the best things might never have come to light. It did come to light through the efforts of Tony and the crazies who were running around at the time, so I guess I'm thankful for that period in a way.'

Bowie's great gift to legions of disaffected British teenagers was the implicit invitation for them to reinvent themselves as he had done – to strike a pose, to revolt into style. After the doldrum years of older brothers' rock, 'the kids' suddenly became a tribe of outlandish freaks, science-fiction peacocks in DIY Ziggy regalia. It was the same stance as the drag queen's self-proclaimed royalty: I may be powerless and sexually outcast, but I am a queen, regal in my deviation. Bolan had started the ball rolling, but Bowie took the 'everybody is a star' aesthetic one stage further. As a Bowie boy or a Bowie girl, you were staking your own claim to autonomy in Edward Heath's grey council-block Britain. People were forced to look – and sometimes to attack.

It couldn't have been more apposite that on the very night when Bowie really cemented his achievement – a show at London's Festival Hall on 8 July 1972 that had *Melody Maker* proclaiming 'A STAR IS BORN' –

Lou Reed made a guest appearance on stage with his disciple, singing 'Waiting for the Man', 'White Light/White Heat' and 'Sweet Jane', with Bowie and the Spiders enthusiastically backing him.

Some of the audience that night would have known that Reed was about to go into the studio to record his second RCA album with Bowie and Ronson. (The first, recorded in London the previous December, had been a less than auspicious solo debut, consisting of Velvets leftovers and lacklustre new songs.) A week after the Festival Hall gig, moreover, Bowie invited both Reed and new MainMan signing Iggy Pop to parade themselves at his Dorchester Hotel press conference – one staged principally for the benefit of a posse of American scribes Tony DeFries had flown in from New York. 'There was booze flowing and a lot of high nervous laughter,' recalled Charles Shaar Murray; 'self-consciousness loose like some predatory gas in the room and just about everyone falling victim to it in their own ways . . .'

The conference was Reed's and Pop's official entrance on to the glam-rock stage. Iggy sported a T. Rex shirt and silver hair, and Reed swanned into the room in platforms and black nail polish, planting a kiss full on Bowie's lips. Reed also donned glitter and mascara for a show that week at London's King's Cross Cinema, sowing the seeds of his 'Phantom of Rock' persona. 'I had seen English bands looking real foppy,' he recalls. 'The Velvets had always dressed in black, but that was partly so we could have things projected on to us. Then things really shifted and I went along with it. When I appeared in London with David doing "White Light", Angie would say, "Oh, Lou, why don't you try wearing something different?" And that was the first time I tried that.' Reed has said that 'the whole glam thing was great' for him: 'It was something I had already seen with Warhol, but I hadn't *done* that thing. The seventies was a chance for me to get in on it, and since no one knew me from Adam particularly, I could say I was anything. I'd learned that from Andy: nobody knows. You could be anything.'

Fittingly, *Transformer* had its inception in a request from Warhol for songs to be used in a Broadway musical based on the Nelson Algren novel *A Walk on the Wild Side*. Warhol had suggested the title 'Vicious', giving rise to *Transformer*'s first song; 'Make Up' and 'New York Telephone Conversation' had followed in swift succession. Eventually,

'Walk on the Wild Side' itself was born – a brilliantly sassy rumination on the Warhol world, boasting name-checks for Factory stars like Candy Darling, Holly Woodlawn and Joe Dallesandro. Like the whole album, 'Wild Side' provided the clearest link between the Factory sixties and the glam seventies, which was precisely what Bowie wanted to achieve with the record. *Transformer*, recorded in the wake of films like *Flesh* (1968) and *Trash* (1970), was the *demi-monde* of the Factory and Max's set to flip, amoral music. 'The glitter people know where I'm at, the gay people know where I'm at,' Reed said. 'I make up songs for them. I was doing things like that in 1966, except people were a lot more uptight then.'

'It was the homosexual time,' wrote Tom Hedley in *Esquire*. 'The faggots were our new niggers. Homosexuality was chic. There was a kind of angry gayness going on and we were very open to making faggots and lesbians our brothers . . . They were the most stylish people in town, they ran the galleries, they had the best clubs, they had the best dinners.' One rock scribe defined 1972 as 'the year of the transsexual tramp'.

Perhaps *Transformer* should have been called *Transformed*, since Bowie was the transformer, the catalyst bringing glam godfather Reed out of the closet. ('*We're coming out/Out of our closets, out on the street*,' Reed sang on 'Make Up'.) If Mick Ronson was the guiding musical light during the sessions at Trident Studios – the same Ronno who had nothing to do with Reed's subterranean world – it was Bowie's take on Reed's milieu that gave *Transformer* its vision and its coherence.

'It was really interesting to see the whole Ziggy thing happening,' says Reed. 'In some ways I took it for granted because of the Warhol scene. But on the other hand, this was not part of the Warhol scene, this was London. So that's what was interesting about it: all these *other* people were running around like that. And I thought it was such fun. What people miss about it is the teenage rebellion and the fun, fun, fun.' A quarter-century after its recording, *Transformer* stands as a key glam artefact, a document of deviance encapsulating the sadistic spirit of Factory cool. 'If [Lou and I] are the spearhead of anything,' Bowie had said at the Dorchester Hotel conference, 'we're not necessarily the spearhead of anything good. Any society that allows people like [us] to become rampant is pretty well lost.'

'It was a convenient thing to duck behind and use as a shield against just about everything,' Reed now says of the ghoulish 'Phantom of Rock' persona he adopted for a good year after the album's release. 'And it was *offered* to me. I didn't have to do anything to get it. In the end it was a strait-jacket and it was very confining – I felt I could do more and write more than that. Of course, I wasn't the only person in New York who looked like that, I just happened to be on stage. The trouble was, I ducked behind the image for so long that after a while there was a real danger of it becoming just a parody thing, where even if I was trying to be serious you didn't know whether to take it seriously or not. There'd been so much posturing that there was a real confusion between that life and real life. I was doing a tightrope act that was pretty scary no matter *where* you were viewing it from.'

While *Transformer* was tracked and Ziggymania gripped the land – Reed hailed Bowie's 19 August show at London's Rainbow as 'the greatest thing I've ever seen' – Ziggy's other mainman was also holed up in a London recording studio. Like Reed, Iggy and the Stooges played the King's Cross Cinema in July – a riotous show which has since gone down in the annals of rock infamy. ('The total effect was more frightening than all the Alice Coopers and *Clockwork Oranges* put together,' noted *NME*'s Nick Kent, 'simply because these guys weren't joking.') Unlike Reed, though, Iggy had politely turned down Bowie's offer to produce an album, saying it was something he had to do himself.

Tony DeFries managed to procure the Stooges the unbelievable sum of £100,000 as an advance from CBS, and it was in CBS's own London studios that the band began recording such maniacal Iggy compositions as 'Gimme Some Skin', '(I'm) Sick of You', 'Tight Pants' and 'Search and Destroy' – a song Iggy wrote stoned on Chinese heroin one afternoon in Kensington Gardens. DeFries, who had wanted the Stooges to do a *Transformer*, with Bowie at the helm, was appalled by the distorted din he heard on the demos for the album. Freaking out, he let them keep only 'Search and Destroy' and the basic riff from 'Tight Pants' (a song subsequently reworked as 'Shake Appeal'). 'So we went in the studio and did the record, one helluva motherfucking record,' said Iggy. 'I don't think anybody from MainMan ever came down to that studio, we just did it ourselves. Bowie was never in the studio. At this point it was pretty much like, "Well, we've got this disaster and let's just let 'em do what they're gonna do . . ."' The result of all this mayhem was the mighty *Raw Power*, released in July 1973 after it had been remixed – dreadfully, in the estimation of many Stooges fans – by Iggy and Bowie. Graced by Mick Rock pictures of the Pop at his glammed-out, transsexual-Jim-Morrison greatest, *Raw Power* was death-trip punk rock, the missing link between the Stones of 'Street Fighting Man' and the Sex Pistols of 'Anarchy in the UK' and a radically different beast from *Ziggy Stardust* or *Transformer*. Twenty-five years later, Iggy himself remixed the album to recapture the quality of what he saw as 'a rip-snortin', super-heavy, nitro-burnin', fuel-injected rock band that nobody in this world could touch at that time', but it was too late to repair the damage done to the Stooges' career by DeFries's prevarication.

DeFries was a good deal more comfortable with another MainMan (and CBS) act, Mott the Hoople. The group had already recorded four Island albums that mixed sludgy, sub-Stones rock 'n' roll ('Walkin' with a Mountain') with rasping, sub-Dylan outings ('Sweet Angeline') before calling it quits after the show later immortalized on 'The Ballad of Mott the Hoople (26 March 1972)'. When David Bowie learned that Mott had broken up he urged them to keep going, offering them 'Suffragette City' and then writing a song that he played for them seated on the floor of Tony DeFries's office.

'I knew immediately that was it,' remembered lead singer Ian Hunter. 'I'd been waiting all my life to hear something like that.' The song was 'All the Young Dudes', and in the summer of 1972 it became *the* anthem of glam rock, a rapturous three-and-a-half-minute call-to-arms for a nation of teenage droogs ignited by Bolan and Bowie.

'*The television man is crazy/Saying we're juvenile delinquent wrecks/Oh man, I need TV when I got T. Rex . . .*'

From the snaking Mick Ralphs guitar line that opens it to Hunter's yelping exhortations on the fade, 'Dudes' was a glorious assertion of pride, a song that shouted, We're young and fast and glittering; we may be gay but we kick like mules; we'll burn out by the time we're twenty-five. The fact that it was sung and performed by a band of West Country boys who'd never so much as flirted with androgyny was beside the point, since it was Bowie's song (you could even hear him singing along in the background chorus). By August it had reached No. 3 on the singles chart, with the *All the Young Dudes* album following close behind. The band could still do honky-tonk rock ('One of the Boys'), but they also did the Velvets' 'Sweet Jane' and Bowie-esque songs like 'Sucker' and 'Sea Diver'.

Were Mott the Hoople a glam band? Not exactly. 'Mott were a bunch of country boys with none of David's sophistication,' says Mick Rock. The young Steven Morrissey was more acerbic: 'For one hysterical split second, they were considered a semi-drag ensemble,' he wrote in his scissors-and-paste monograph on the New York Dolls. 'But they confessed, *"Don't wanna be hip/But thanks for the great trip."'* If Mott partially embraced camp – particularly in the get-ups of bassist Overend Watts – their latent homophobia and fundamental chauvinism were only too obvious in Ian Hunter's passing remarks about 'fag rock' in his *Diary of a Rock 'n' Roll Star*. 'It's a bit upsetting to watch guys who you've played with before . . . who were hard-driving and straight, turn poovy,' Hunter wrote of Brownsville Station, the support act at a Philadelphia date on 29 November 1972.[1]

So what did Bowie see in this cut-price Faces with Les Paul riffs, Al Kooper organ chords and a fucked-up-Dylan lead voice? Possibly not what he saw in Lou Reed and Iggy Pop. Well, if it was nothing more than a vehicle for a timeless glam anthem, then it was all worth it.

'Boogaloo dudes/Carry the news . . .'

[1] Amusing to note that in the very same entry, Hunter reports how David Bowie 'enthusiastically speaks of the New York Dolls'.

all that glitters

'It was a brilliant pop era, wasn't it? The last proper pop era, probably . . .'

Mickie Most

Glam's Leiber and Stoller: Nicky Chinn (left) and Mike Chapman

'The Day Pop Came Back!' roared a newspaper headline on 19 March 1972, the morning after T. Rex played a historic sell-out show at the

Empire Pool in Wembley. T. Rexstasy was now official, with Bolan hailed as the fantasy idol of countless glitter girls and boys. 'I've never seen so many beautiful fourteen-year-old girls in my life as at the T. Rex Wembley concert,' reported Charles Shaar Murray in *Creem*. Even when Marc reverted to acoustic elfin-princeling mode and warbled 'Cosmic Dancer' sitting cross-legged on the floor, the fourteen-year-olds roared their approval.

Things were going even better for Bolan in 1972 than they had in 1971: two genius No. 1s in 'Telegram Sam' and 'Metal Guru', a solid album in *The Slider* and the likeable Ringo Starr-produced film *Born to Boogie* just in time for Christmas. Now, however, there was serious competition in the form of David Bowie, whose fusion of teen pop and art rock could never have happened without T. Rex. And Bowie wasn't the only artist Bolan had inspired.

'Bolan started the whole glam-rock thing,' said producer Mike Leander, the Svengali behind Gary Glitter and the Glitter Band. 'He put glitter on his eyelids, then added a pencil line and mascara. He wore a velvet jacket with an ostrich feather boa flung around his neck. Glam rock was all about putting on a spectacle. The records, too, were constructed to be seen, whereas in the sixties they were constructed to be heard, preferably with a joint dangling from your lip. The glam audience became part of the show. They dressed up and it was like a party. Bowie succeeded best because he took it further musically. His records were tailored towards a slightly older audience, while Gary's and Bolan's catchment was the eight- to fifteen-year-olds.'

'Bolan was without a doubt the start,' says Nicky Chinn, who co-wrote umpteen glam hits for the Sweet and Suzi Quatro. 'He was the forerunner. I remembered seeing him with Tyrannosaurus Rex and the transition was unbelievable. No question, when "Ride a White Swan" appeared on the scene, both Mike and I went, "Hey, that is something unbelievable, something very, very special." I don't think there was a sense at that point that glam could be a fully fledged thing, but nor did we think it was a fad that would just come and go. At that time, the focus tended to be on the records and the music. No one was taking any great notice of the image. Bolan was just making great records, and if he wanted to look like that he could. The marketing men hadn't taken over the pop industry at that point. You had *Top of the Pops* once a week, but other than that there was very little visual. No money was being spent on marketing, and "image" almost wasn't a word that was being used. Image was something that just happened. Take Elvis: his image was unbelievable, but I don't think anybody worked on it other than him. It was the same with Bolan.'

For Chinn, the next indication that anything big was bubbling under the surface came in the form of a bunch of Brummie oiks who'd formed, and even recorded, back in the mid-sixties. Changing their name from the 'N Betweens to Ambrose Slade, they were taken on by Jimi Hendrix manager Chas Chandler, became skinheads and (as Slade) released 1970s boot-stomping 'Wild Winds are Blowing'. Even after the glam makeover that followed the raucous 'Get Down and Get Down with It' (1971), Slade looked like hooligan clowns – goofy guitarist Dave Hill actually had the legend SUPERYOB emblazoned on his guitar. In October of that year, the group released 'Coz I Luv You', an eccentric record which sounded like Family's Roger Chapman fronting a gypsy string band, and found themselves at No. 1. (The title's misspelling, a feature of their many hits over the ensuing two years, gleefully flaunted their oafishness.) Who would ever forget their first glimpse of singer Neville 'Noddy' Holder's fulsome bugger grips, or of Dave Hill's hilarious fringed Mullet? For all their glam togs, there was precious little that was effeminate about Slade. Many more would follow in the group's clodhopping footsteps, from the Sweet to the Spiders from Mars to Arthur Harold Kane of the New York Dolls: brickies in eyeliner seemed almost as endemic to glam as swishing queens.

Slade, in the words of Michael Bracewell, were all about 'stomping out the hippie sensitivity and pedantic virtuosity of Yes or Emerson, Lake & Palmer with their impudently caricatured platform boots'. As Noddy Holder himself opined, 'The fans are fed up with paying to sit on their hands while watching musicians who clearly couldn't care less about the customers.' While older brothers (and even older sisters) became prog fiends or deadheads, teenage Britain awoke from its bubblegum slumbers and started grooving to the crass beats and chunky Gibson chords of a pop sound which had at last had a bit of party-time flash injected into it. If Slade's records weren't exactly masterpieces, they were, as Stephen Barnard wrote at the time, 'celebrations of teenage community', explosions of unbridled rock energy that teenagers could stomp to as they groped each other in the dark. '*Cum on feel the noize/Girls grab the boys . . .*'

The Sweet had been going almost as long as Slade when they heaved themselves aboard the glam bandwagon in 1971. Unlike Slade, however, they came out of bubblegum, despite harbouring secret hard-rock/metal aspirations. 'The pop scene was very unexciting in early 1971,' concedes Nicky Chinn. 'It was very bland and in a tremendous lull. It was the Tony Macaulay, Roger Cook and Roger Greenaway era. All terrific writers, but very soft, very bubblegum. When we looked at directions to go in, we thought of those guys and what they were doing; we thought of "Love Grows (Where My Rosemary Goes)" and "Gimme Dat Ding", and "Sugar Sugar" in America – it was no coincidence that we wrote "Funny Funny" [Sweet's first hit in early 1971] after that. People were waiting for something to happen, even if it was a subconscious kind of waiting.'

Chinn had met Mike Chapman at Tramp, a hotspot for London pop people ever since its opening in Jermyn Street in late 1969. Chapman was waiting tables at the club and playing in a pop group called Tangerine Peel; Chinn was already writing songs with the ex-Manfred Mann singer Mike D'Abo. For Sweet the duo wrote a string of bubblegum hits – including the No. 2 smash 'Co-Co' in June 1971 – before going glam with 'Wigwam Bam' in September 1972. 'How much influence did Marc Bolan have?' says Chinn. 'We never said, let's copy Marc Bolan, but the fact that he happened must have opened a big door. And then Slade began to happen. And then of course Bowie started doing some of that and without doubt opened another door. And by no means to be forgotten was the pushing of Sweet themselves, who were not that happy with the "Funny Funny"s and "Co-Co"s and "Poppa Joe"s. Once they'd had them, and had had hits, then there was definitely some pushing from them, that this was not really what they wanted to be.'

The beefed-up, turbo-charged 'Chinnichap' sound – bubblepunk, one might almost call it – reached its apex on the great Sweet hits of 1973–4, from the chart-topping 'Blockbuster!' to the wild 'Teenage

Rampage'. As a formula it was unapologetically trashy, with the songs churned out at top speed in Chinn's Hill Street flat and meticulously moulded at Island or Audio International studios by Chapman. 'The sound was designed, and it had to be right,' says Chinn. 'It was more contrived than Bowie, without a doubt. But we were very conscious of giving pop back to the kids, and giving them something to smile about and bop to and generally get off on. Maybe this was part of the age of *not* having to interpret, of just having fun. There was no hidden agenda: pop should be fun and this is what we want you to have. Now, of course, the records sound quite raw and punky – there are people who say Sweet were the first punk band! And although I say it wasn't to be taken too seriously, there was something about bubblegum that couldn't be taken seriously *at all*, whereas this was pop that had an edge: there *were* hard guitars, there *were* crashing drums. There was *some* Led Zeppelin in there.'

The combination of blow-dried, golden-maned frontman Brian Connolly and pouting, be-caped bassist Steve Priest would prove to be a regular fixture in the charts and on *Top of the Pops*. 'No one suggested that Steve become the camp one, it totally came from within him,' says Chinn. 'Those rather outrageous one-liners that he did, from "Wigwam Bam" onwards, were the thing that gave him a front-of-stage part. The story I always remember the best was the one that summed up what the Sweet were doing. We were doing "Ballroom Blitz" on *Top of the Pops*, and all day Steve had been acting a bit strangely. After the opening bars of the song, he turns round with his back to the camera, and on the back of his leather jacket were the words FUCK YOU. Well, you couldn't *do* that on *Top of the Pops*! Robin Nash, the producer, was down the stairs like a whippet. And would you believe it, this fucking band starts to argue with him! And he says, "Look, you either take that off or you're off the show." I had one minute to persuade Steve to get rid of the jacket. And maybe that sums up glam rock, because there was this harder side to what was going on, but ultimately they had to compromise.'[1]

1 It's easy to forget that, three years before punk rock, Steve Priest actually wore a swastika armband – together with a Hitler pencil moustache – on *Top of the Pops*.

On the side, Chinn and Chapman were also writing songs for the acts on Mickie Most's RAK label, from the middle-of-the-road New World ('Tom Tom Turnaround') to the fast-lane Suzi Quatro. 'The first I knew of Suzi was this little girl who'd come over from Detroit and would sit in the top office at RAK in Charles Street, strumming away on her bass and writing songs, drinking an awful lot of black coffee and smoking an awful lot of cigarettes and eating nothing,' chuckles Chinn. 'We got to know Suzi very well. Mickie made an album with her of her songs and it came to nothing, so he called me up one day and asked if we'd write a song for her . . . and we wrote "Can the Can", and it went to No. 1.'

Quatro was glam in reverse: twice as butch as the male stars of the era, she was a feisty Motor City moll who'd played in her sister's garage band the Pleasure Seekers before catching the riveted eyes of Mickie Most. In 1972 Quatro took Most up on his offer to bring her to London: 'I put her into a small hotel and kind of anglicized her,' he recalled. It took the magic Chinnichap touch, however, to propel the girl chartwards. On *Top of the Pops*, Quatro and band looked like pop-art bikers: Suzi's trademark was her black-leather catsuit, which she occasionally swapped for a gold one. 'I feel funny in dresses and skirts,' she vouchsafed. 'The guys in my band don't wear glitter – they're *real* men.' Like Sweet, Quatro was pure camp: you couldn't take her seriously as a hard rocker, even though (in the classic Susan Sontag formulation) she *proposed* herself seriously as hard rock.[2]

When it came to camp, though, neither Sweet nor Suzi Quatro could hold a candle to Gary Glitter, the most comically outrageous star glam ever produced. Performance artist Paul Gadd (a.k.a. Paul Raven) went all the way back to the days of skiffle and Hamburg, and was well over thirty when he and veteran pop producer Mike Leander sat down one day and dreamed up the *alter ego* Gary Glitter.

'Mike and Gary had known each other for years,' says Laurence

2 Would there have been a Joan Jett, or even a Chrissie Hynde, without Suzi Quatro? Rock's many male impersonators owe the former Pleasure Seeker a huge debt; Jett even made the debt to glam explicit with her massively successful cover of 'I Love Rock 'n' Roll', by RAK act the Arrows.

Myers, who managed both men. 'Mike had dragged me down to see Paul Raven and urged me to manage him, but I felt he couldn't sing. Anyway, Mike had made this record with Gary called "Rock and Roll", and me being cheap, instead of recording a new B-side we left the voice track up, whacked on a bit of guitar and called it "Rock and Roll Part 2". We then decided on the Superman image, because Gary was very butch – to Mike Leander goes the credit for this glittery, tinselly, almost sci-fi superhero image. We called him Gary Glitter, didn't think a lot about it, and then a DJ went and turned the record over. Next thing we know, we're on *Top of the Pops*, and Gary has to go on stage without any vocals. Very few other people in the world could have carried it off. And that was the launch of Glitter. The name became synonymous with glitter and glam rock.'

If Slade and Sweet were crass, then 'Rock and Roll Part 2' was mind-numbingly dumb. But therein lay its strange, stupid genius: it was Slade meets Bowie, football chant meets future rock. And Gary – glam's wicked Uncle Ernie from outer space – was, in his schlocky way, as much of a showman as Bolan or Bowie. With his grotesque hair and bulging eyes, he was part panto dame, part rhinestone Elvis, part *Doctor Who* Time Lord. 'If you'd asked me at the time what connection there was between Iggy Pop and Gary Glitter, I'd have said none whatsoever,' says Laurence Myers. 'But the thing that binds it all together is the androgyny, the camping it up. It's what Marc started, and what Bowie did with that. Gary may not have been androgynous, but he was certainly camping it up. I've never seen such a heterosexual group as the Sweet, but they all got into the make-up, with the stars on their faces and the pouting. It wasn't the music, it wasn't the musical influences. It was this very camp thing, and it was the artists who did it. It wasn't some manager saying, "Y'know what we need to do?" It was done *in spite of* the reservations, and even the horror, of managers and record companies. So then all the kids would go around wearing make-up, and it was fine; it was healthy and it was terrific.'

'Looking back on it,' David Bowie told Suede's Brett Anderson in 1993, 'we were a very odd little genre. Because – to knock out Sweet and all of that – there were actually only a very few of us working. What became known as glam or glitter rock wasn't a movement at all, musically. It was very limited. On this side of the Atlantic there was myself, Roxy, Bolan and to a certain extent Slade, I guess.'

Between Laurence Myers's GTO, Mickie Most's RAK and Dick Leahy's Bell Records (to which Gary Glitter was signed), the London glitter-pop sound was pretty much sewn up. 'The interchange was enormous,' says Nicky Chinn. 'Bell was right next door to RAK on Charles Street, and we were all friends. It was friendly competition. We would play each other the records that were coming out. What was going on in that street in those two offices was quite influential, and very exciting. And I think it had a tremendous amount to do with what was going on in *our* circle.'

'We were the people responsible for telling the kids what they were going to buy,' said the more Machiavellian Mike Chapman. 'Not asking them what they wanted, but telling them, and it worked. We were like a little gang in those days, and we actually used to schedule our releases so we wouldn't interfere with each other's No. 1s.' (According to his son Calvin Hayes, Mickie Most put Mud's 'Tiger Feet' on the RAK release schedule on the strength of the title alone; the song itself hadn't even been written.) The prefab aspect of glitter pop was part of its charm. 'We don't go picking up products just for the sake of it,' claimed Dick Leahy. 'We always ask first, "Who's going to buy it?" If we can't answer that question we don't release the record.' A pop song, said Mickie Most, is 'something that takes fifteen minutes to make and two weeks to forget'.

Inevitably, this aesthetic of disposability made Chinnichap pop a pet hate among music writers in their twenties. 'The music press looked down on us greatly, apart from *Record Mirror*,' says Chinn. 'Some ghastly things were said about us. I remember Bryan Ferry knocking us, and I was quite upset at the time. But I also thought, what the hell's *he* got to knock us about? I think we were probably looked down on because our bands weren't writing their own songs, but on the other hand there may have been some envy involved because we were having bigger hits. Yet at the same time I remember going to a Led Zeppelin party at Peter Grant's place, and they kept on playing "Ballroom Blitz". So I went up to Robert Plant and said, "Do me a favour, stop taking the piss," and he said, "This is one of our favourite records!" Zeppelin were so big that they could afford to appreciate *anything*. They didn't have that snobbery.'

Time, of course, has vindicated Chinn and Most and Glitter and the rest of the glitter clique. Where countless bands in patched loon pants and centre partings have disappeared into rock's black hole, Sweet and Gary Glitter live on, charming new pop generations with their doltish classics.

One of the biggest records of summer 1972 was 'School's Out' by Alice Cooper. Supercharged and leeringly evil, it caught the crazed frenzy of adolescent life at a crucial point in the early seventies. In Britain it got to No. 1.

'No more teachers, dirty looks . . .'

Having fallen in love with Bolan and Bowie, I myself wasn't sure where to place Cooper in the glam scheme of things. Alice's problem was that he didn't look like a teen rebel. He looked too old and ghoulish, too Hammer horror by half. Significantly, he was being slagged off by British glam rockers six months before 'School's Out' was even released. 'I think he's *trying* to be outrageous,' David Bowie told Michael Watts in a scathing assessment. 'You can see him, poor dear, with his red eyes sticking out and his temples straining. He tries so hard. That bit he does with the boa constrictor, a friend of mine – Rudy Valentino – was doing ages before. The next thing I see is Miss C with her boa. I find him very demeaning. It's very premeditated, but quite fitting with our era. He's probably more successful than I am at present, but I've invented a new category of artist, with my chiffon and taff. They call it pantomime rock in the States.'[3]

On 1 January 1973, on *The Old Grey Whistle Test*, Bob Harris asked the American producer/scenemaker Kim Fowley to define the difference between Bowie and Cooper. Fowley replied that Bowie

---

3 Bowie hadn't changed his mind on this matter when he talked to Brett Anderson in 1993. 'Alice Cooper were just a rock band who wore mascara,' he said. 'I don't think they even tried theatricality until they saw the English bands. It felt to us that they were more Frank Zappa than part of this compunction to parody rock and make it very vaudeville or whatever it was that some of us were doing.'

was Rommel and Cooper was Eisenhower – that Bowie was an innovator and Cooper an imitator. The analogy was a fair one, even if Cooper has had an unfairly bad rap in the glam-rock chronicles. Compared to Bowie, or to Iggy Pop, Cooper's act was mere theatre, far removed from true outrage. Where Iggy was usually to be found semi-comatose in the Max's Kansas City toilet, the Cooper band would be found conscientiously applying their make-up in the dressing room.

'Alice is really so straight when he's off stage, a typical suburban punk,' noted Max's Kansas City stalwart Danny Fields. Slowly, moreover, Cooper moved from shock-value transvestism to Gothic overkill. 'Alice Cooper had to stop wearing ladies' sling-back shoes and false eyelashes and dresses and get more into horror,' sneered Jayne County. 'People could understand horror and blood and dead babies, but they couldn't understand male/female sexuality, androgyny or, as little American boys would say, fag music.'

Cooper, born Vince Furnier, had initially been adopted by Frank Zappa as one of the 'freak' acts on his Straight Records roster. Like the Stooges, the band defined themselves by their hatred of hippies; perhaps it was no great surprise when they shifted base from Hollywood to Cooper's hometown, Detroit. Playing undistinguished garage metal – there was nothing of the Stooges' animal frenzy or the MC5's political blitzkrieg in their sound[4] – they recorded two laughable albums before hooking up with Canadian producer Bob Ezrin for the vast improvement that was 1971's *Love It to Death*. Ezrin set about grafting some real musicality on to the band's grungy base, an immediate result being the brilliantly anthemic '(I'm) Eighteen': '*I'm in the middle without any plans/I'm a boy and I'm a man,*' Cooper sang on the track, a

---

4 Note, by the way, that the MC5's 1970 album *Back in the USA* was a very different animal from the incendiary live masterpiece *Kick out the Jams*. Full of spunky two-and-a-half-minute classics like 'Tonight', 'High School' and 'Teenage Lust', *Back in the USA* was a supercharged garage-pop album that boldly rejected the long-winded 'jamming' ethos of late sixties ballroom rock. The 5 may not have been glam, but on this album they came closer to glam rock than even the Stooges did.

Top Thirty hit in America. *'I'm eighteen and I don't know what to do . . .'*[5]

By the time Cooper hit the road in May 1971, the band's image was lurching towards glam, or at least a Gothic version of glam. Cooper painted spider's-web circles around his eyes, and the group (who were even less effeminate than Slade) donned Lurex jumpsuits. Overshadowing the apparel and the mascara, however, was all the paraphernalia they took on the road, from dismemberable dolls to electric chairs to Kachina the boa constrictor. With *Killer*, released at the end of the year, the group established itself as a horror-movie freak show, with songs like 'Dead Babies' becoming centrepieces of their gigs. The show would climax with Cooper being hung from a gallows by neanderthal-looking guitarist Glen Buxton.

'Alice didn't take any drugs and was never into shagging groupies,' remembered Bebe Buell, whose then beau Todd Rundgren supported Cooper on tour. 'You could go to him with your problems and he would be really sweet and patient, but he liked TV and Budweiser. I felt so sorry for that poor snake, but Todd would always say, "Don't worry about it. The snake has been on the road for a long time. The snake drinks, the snake smokes, the snake has girlfriends – he gets laid more than any of us."'

The *School's Out* album, full of songs about fisticuffs and high-school feuding, was more sophisticated but less satisfying than *Killer*. 'I think it was a bit overproduced, with the horns and stuff,' noted the band's principal tunesmith Michael Bruce in his *No More Mr Nice Guy* (1996). 'It was such a drastic leap from the hard edge of *Killer*. I'm sure a lot of fans were turned off by it. It was a very vaudeville type of record.' *Rolling*

---

5 However inauthentic Cooper may have seemed to the glam élite of London and New York, it's easy to underestimate what he meant to suburban misfits in America at large. 'I liked the whole theatrical glitter thing he was doing,' remembered Joey Ramone, 'and [the fact] that he was very primal, like Iggy and the Stooges, which brought out the beast in me. I really believed in Alice until I found out he wasn't really a necrophiliac . . .' Sonic Youth's Thurston Moore remembers sitting in the school cafeteria when a group of Yes fans converged on him and demanded to know what sort of music he liked. When he told them he liked Alice Cooper, they sniggered at him. 'I knew these guys were jerks,' said Moore. 'I knew that I had an intellectual edge over them.'

Stone's reviewer Ben Gerson adjudged that the album was 'as aimless musically as it is lyrically', adding that he was waiting for David Bowie – 'a more credible transvestite' – to break through Stateside. Michael Bruce counters that the Cooper band 'had never really wanted to be seen as transvestites, credible or otherwise' and that they 'never thought of [themselves] as being a glam band like Sweet or Slade'. And Philip Cato was right to say – in his enjoyable *Crash Course for the Ravers* (1997) – that *School's Out* was worth having 'simply for Alice's Budweiser-frazzled vision of America as seen through the eyes of a man who seemed to cop most of his influences from TV and comic books'.

The truth is that Alice Cooper was nothing more than a competent hard-rock act that achieved notoriety through the tackiest kind of *Grand Guignol* but managed to make some good records thanks to a talented producer. (It was ironic that Lou Reed, who was among Cooper's detractors, wound up working with Bob Ezrin on *Berlin*, the mordant follow-up to *Transformer*.) In this respect he was no different from other essentially mainstream acts who found themselves – willingly or unwillingly – on board the glam gravy train. Acts like Rod Stewart, who flung on a few glam clothes and sported a 'feather' (or 'shag') haircut that proved hugely influential; like Elton John, a pudgy piano man from Pinner who revamped himself as a glam Liberace; like Queen, who were to ballsy hard-rock quartets what Elton was to sensitive piano-playing singer-songwriters; or even like the Rolling Stones, who broke out the make-up box again on their 1972 American tour and went very fey to promote 1973's 'Angie'. 'Glamour' began to pervade pop after the emergence of Bolan and Bowie and the glitter groups. If you didn't make some concession to it you looked like a frump.

'*If you know how to rock/You don't have to shock*,' Marc Bolan sang on the sub-par *Tanx*, released in March 1973. It was, he said, his response to 'that glam-rock crap stuff' – the glitter-by-numbers teeny pop he was hearing all around him as 1972 rolled into 1973.

'I used [the song] against the so-called glam rock, which I appear to be buttoned up with, and which I don't necessarily believe in at all,' he said. 'I mean, I believe in music and the clothes I wear, but the attitude I have had since I was ten. So that's what the song is saying – if you can rock it doesn't really matter if you wear pink satin trousers and a feather boa. Glam rock is sham rock. Elvis Presley was doing it fifteen years ago and Hedy Lamarr was doing it too! So was Gloria Swanson!'

After the last great T. Rex single, 'The Groover', came out in June 1973, Bolan expanded on this theme. 'I didn't want to get sucked into second-generation glam rock,' he said. 'I did that thing for a year and then after the concert at Wembley [in March 1972] there was nowhere to go except Earls Court and that seemed to have been a disaster for everybody. I felt slightly overexposed in the papers, so I thought I'd back off. I figured I could see what was happening. My next thing won't be glam rock. I'm telling you that, babe. I don't want to be involved in any of that. [. . .] I wore gold suits and that sort of shit for a while, but it was a flash. Billy Fury wore them four years before; it wasn't an innovation. I don't put down anyone who is involved in it, but once the vision takes over from the music they're in bad shape.'

Bolan's central problem, exacerbated by his use of cocaine, was that he lacked the vision to move beyond glam. Gold suits or no gold suits, his music was deteriorating terribly. 'Sadly, Marc would never develop further than the three-minute single,' says Tony Visconti. 'He could have, and he did on his earlier Tyrannosaurus Rex things, but he never carried a lot of that over into his rock phase. I wish he had. With David, the glam rock smoothly segued into a kind of art rock.'

If Bolan was unhappy about being associated with Sweet and Gary Glitter, Bowie was positively mortified about it. 'It actually became a sense of embarrassment, iconically,' he said. 'I mean, in my feather boas and dresses, I certainly didn't wanna be associated with the likes of Gary Glitter, who was obviously a charlatan.' To Suede's Brett Anderson he said that 'we were very miffed that people who'd obviously never seen *Metropolis* and had never heard of Christopher Isherwood were actually becoming glam rockers'.[6] This was at least

6 Ironically, 'The Jean Genie' – a song purportedly about Iggy Pop while playing on the name Jean Genet – borrowed exactly the same Yardbirds riff as Sweet's 'Blockbuster!'. Adding insult to injury, 'Blockbuster!' went on to keep 'Jean Genie' off the No. 1 spot in January 1973. 'Because Bowie was hipper than Sweet, the tendency was to infer that we'd ripped off Bowie,' says Nicky Chinn. 'I remember being introduced to Bowie at Tramp at that very time, and he looked up at me completely deadpan and said, "Cunt!" And then he got up and gave me a hug and said, "Congratulations . . ."'

partly why, in 1973, Bowie decided to kill off Ziggy Stardust.

First he created a new persona, a modified Ziggy, in the form of Aladdin Sane. The 'lad insane' was the Ziggy/Bowie who found himself travelling vast distances across north America on a US tour in late 1972, his mind teeming with cartoon visions of catastrophe. The songs turned America – the America of 'Panic in Detroit' and 'Drive-in Saturday' – into a surreal, polysexual playground, a nation of neon and Quaaludes, a place at once depraved and coldly alienating. The mood was not unlike that of *The Man Who Sold the World*, with more aggressive arrangements and decidedly showier playing – especially in the baroque tinkling of pianist Mike Garson.

Aladdin Sane was less focused, and more unhinged, than *Ziggy Stardust*: it suggested a mind teetering on the edge of psychosis, writing under intense pressure, writhing beneath the spotlight of media attention. 'This decadence thing is just a bloody joke,' Bowie told *Melody Maker* in May 1973. 'I'm very normal [. . .] I never thought Ziggy would become the most talked-about man in the world. I never thought it would become that unreal [. . .] I felt somewhat like a Dr Frankenstein.'

Exhausted by a long tour that had taken him back to America, to Japan and to Europe, Bowie made the apparently spontaneous decision to retire Ziggy and the Spiders as the band wound up the last show of the tour at the Hammersmith Odeon. *'Making love with his ego/Ziggy sucked up into his mind,'* he had sung on 'Ziggy Stardust'. *'Like a leper messiah/When the kids had killed the man I had to break up the band.'* Watching D. A. Pennebaker's film of the concert, the fatigue of the cracked actor is all too obvious under his caked make-up and gauzy, fan-like costumes: all the glam in the world can't conceal Bowie's heavy sockets, sheer cheekbones and bad teeth. Next to Mick Ronson, an *ingenu* stud in glitter and breeches, Ziggy is epicene to the point of anorexia. When Angie Bowie sticks her head round the door of her husband's dressing room, it's like eavesdropping on a ghost. Perhaps the most revealing song of the night is Brel's 'My Death'.

After a supercharged 'Suffragette City' and a 'White Light/White Heat' prefaced by the remark 'I *think* [Lou Reed's] a friend of mine',

Bowie announced that this was 'the last show we'll ever do', then serenaded his bewildered followers with a beseeching version of 'Rock 'n' Roll Suicide'.

Ziggy Stardust, pop martyr, had fallen to earth.

the lives of bryan and brian

'Besides, what's real and what's make believe?'
Roxy Music

The original Roxy Music: (left to right) Andy Mackay, Paul Thompson, Phil Manzanera, Bryan Ferry (seated), Brian Eno

A man even more miffed than Bowie and Bolan at being lumped together with the clowns of glitter pop was Bryan Ferry of Roxy Music. For Ferry, who had studied with the pop artist Richard Hamilton, using 'glamour' in rock was a conceptual device, not simply a vehicle for eye-catching entertainment.

'There was a very strong difference between early Roxy and the glam-rock thing,' said Roxy sleeve designer Nick de Ville, who'd also been a pupil of Hamilton's. 'There were some people who were trapped in that as a style, like Gary Glitter, for instance, who's still doing it as a fantastic pastiche of himself. And there were others, pre-eminently Roxy, who adopted it in a strategic way for a while until it no longer seemed interesting. That temporary adoption of style and persona was something very much proposed by Richard Hamilton.'

Roxy were glam for adults – or at least for smart, savvy students. Like Bowie, Roxy brought brains to the glam-rock party, bridging the gap between progressive 'art' rock and disposable teen pop. Like him, they understood that taking the avant-garde into the high street was a more radical, 'progressive' goal than continuing to operate within the denim ghetto that was polytechnic rock. 'We didn't feel much connection with the Sweet or Gary Glitter,' says Brian Eno, 'but I think all of those things were a sort of reaction to what had happened immediately before, which was an idea of musicianship where you turned your back on the audience and got into your guitar solo. I think all of those bands – us and Bowie and the others – were turning round towards the audience and saying, "We are doing a show." In that sense there was a unity, though it wasn't very obvious at the time.'

Unlike Bowie, Roxy drew as much on the past as on the future, fusing cheap science fiction with iconic Hollywood melodrama. Ferry was obsessed with the camp and kitsch that surrounded the great movie legends. 'I certainly felt a need to present the music we were doing in a glamorous way,' he says. 'Maybe I was watching the wrong movies when I was brought up, liking that kind of showiness! The irony is that all the people in Roxy were non-pushy, retiring types.' The result was a kind of retro-futurism that combined thirties glamour with fifties grease and twenty-first-century plasticity.[1]

'I had quite a good working knowledge of different kinds of pop music,' says Ferry. 'Nearly all of it was American, although I was also a fan of Lotte Lenya and Piaf, and there were certain European things that filtered through as well. So there was a lot of history, looking backwards as well as forwards, because I think that's how people advance – one step back, two forwards. There was more affinity with Bowie than with Bolan, but we felt very different even from him. He seemed to have been around a bit, and his band seemed very old-fashioned. It was all very straightforward music, even though he was dressed up in a very extreme way. I think that's what made it such a big success in America, that he had those conventional weapons. It wasn't over their heads, whereas when we went to America we went totally over their heads.'

Bowie, who was supported by Roxy when he played the Rainbow in August 1972, saw both the parallels and the differences. 'Myself and Roxy were very aware of what we were doing,' he said. 'Eno [. . . was] very aware of breaking down the barriers between high and low art. I can't speak for either Brian/Bryan, but I don't think any of us felt there was a movement or any unified culture. Because all that had fragmented by the time the seventies began.'

Breaking down the barriers between high and low art: not a bad description of what Roxy Music were doing in the golden glam year of 1972.

Roxy had been formed after Ferry and bass guitarist Graham Simpson, survivors of a Tyneside R&B band called the Gas Board, began questing for musical accomplices in London in late 1970. The first real recruit was the temperamental ex-Nice guitarist Davey O'List, who stayed until early 1972. Classically trained oboeist Andy Mackay arrived in January 1971, bringing with him fellow avant-gardist Brian Peter George St John le Baptiste de la Salle Eno. 'Eno wasn't at all flamboyant when we first met him,' remembers Ferry. 'He was very

1 Like Bowie, Ferry had been fascinated by Andy Warhol and the Factory. Roxy's debut single, 'Virginia Plain', was based on a painting Ferry had done several years earlier, and reflected what he called 'a whole American dream thing, living up in Newcastle yet constantly thinking about Warhol's Factory and Baby Jane Holzer . . .'

sober – if anyone had a joint in the room he'd start getting giddy. His flat was a boffin's paradise: wires everywhere, bits of old speakers.'

'He had long hair and he had an almost mad-professor look,' says Simon Puxley, who'd known both Mackay and Eno in the late sixties – and who would become Roxy's publicist. 'He had been the Social Sec at Winchester Arts College. The flamboyance came later – it was being in Roxy that brought it out, and quite extraordinarily. But he was never quiet. He was very good at selling himself and his ideas.'

'I was very impressed by the music,' says Eno. 'It sounded to me like something quite new and different. I'd never thought of joining a band, but I just thought, this is the most fun I've ever had. I think Bryan had written most of the first record. "Virginia Plain" came much later, but most of the songs on the album we played for about a year and a half before we ever even played live. There was a long, long period of just rehearsing these things and going over and over them. Which actually I think was rather unusual.

'I saw the songs in the context of pop art. That was the period when pop music became sort of self-conscious, in the sense that it started to look at its own history as material that could be used. One of the things we didn't like about the bands that had preceded us was that they were so unironic, they were so serious about what they were doing. We were serious, but in a different way. We wanted to also say, "We know we're working in pop music, we know there's a history to it, and we know it's a showbiz game. And knowing all that we're still going to try to do something new."'

Eno had been very influenced by the Velvet Underground, and wanted to import that group's 'consciousness' into Roxy Music. 'It wasn't simply a mood thing, it was that rock music could be about complicated and ambiguous and mixed-up moods. Which I think Bryan already had – that was the strongest part of his writing. It was also to do with the idea that rock music could be part of the cutting edge of culture as we knew it, not just about music but art in general. That was the other message of the Velvets, and it was also why I liked the Who.'

'Looking back, Eno was the strongest person for me to bounce off, even though he didn't play,' says Ferry. 'He was much more opinionated than the others.' Initially, Eno was simply the band's 'sound man', mixing the group from the back of the stage while producing a variety of deranged bleeps and squeaks from Andy Mackay's VCS3 synthesizer. Only later did he graduate to official Roxy membership. 'They moved him on stage, and since Bryan was stage right they used Eno as a counterbalance on stage left,' says David Enthoven, who co-managed the group. 'Eno on stage meant that Bryan didn't have to play piano.'

Although Ferry at this point had written only a handful of songs, he was already full of dreams and schemes. 'He had no grand plan, though I wouldn't deny he was very ambitious,' recalled Andy Mackay, who was soon practising R&B solos on a new saxophone. Anchoring Roxy by this time was an unpretentious Geordie drummer named Paul Thompson, a mascara'd brickie in the Slade tradition. The final piece of the jigsaw — like the Doors, Roxy couldn't seem to settle on a permanent bass player — was fitted when Havana-born guitarist Phil Manzanera replaced O'List in February 1972.

By the time the band started playing live, it was clear that their look was going to be as important as their sound. 'I was much more into the tailored side of things, and that's where Antony Price was great,' says Ferry. 'There was a harder edge, working in elements of American gangster style. It had more cross-referencing for me. You'd get bits of Raymond Chandler coming in, or bits of Fred Astaire. I liked patent-leather shoes and artistry, not people just glumly standing around with long hair — I wasn't interested in that. Antony I saw at a party in about 1971, just before it all started. He was working at Stirling Cooper in Wigmore Street — the in place, with exciting design, tight trousers and big shoulders, very sexy looks.' Price himself has claimed that he was 'obsessed with the ultimate Jayne Mansfield female, the *Girl Can't Help It* look, vastly different to all these hooray waifs stoned out of their heads in little flimsy see-through frocks'. He wanted to create 'buxom, powerful women' and 'males with shorn-off hair, with ears showing and quiffs'.

Out of the various themes and motifs that Ferry and Price pooled, the retro-futurist look quickly evolved. 'There was a lot of kitsch in there, a lot of Americana,' says David Enthoven. 'It was Bryan's dream. Antony obviously had a hand in realizing it, and Nick de Ville, but the vision was all Bryan's. The whole thing was music and packaging.' When *Melody Maker*'s Richard Williams saw Roxy play a small gig at London's 100 Club, what he described as 'a ready-made audience of girls in pill-box hats and tight skirts' was already in attendance. The record companies weren't so convinced. 'I felt Roxy were very much outsiders, and that was quite exciting,' says Simon Puxley. 'I remember feeling that we were regarded as pretty weird by record companies, and I also remember not caring.'

'Island was hardly a likely home for a glam act,' says Tim Clark, then the label's marketing director. 'T. Rex, for example, was pop music, and we didn't particularly want to get involved – we actually turned Bolan down. We had the wonderfully flamboyant thing with Emerson, Lake & Palmer, and the bluesy thing with Free and Traffic. It was college rock, if you like, and there was a great college circuit where all these bands played. I'm not sure what Bryan thought his roots were, but they probably had more to do with Marilyn Monroe than with any musical influences. What was certainly the case is that Bryan and Roxy took something that might have been pop but actually had as much to do with King Crimson. It was certainly not teeny bop.'

In the end, *Roxy Music* was entirely financed by EG Management, who not only looked after Emerson, Lake & Palmer and King Crimson but had represented T. Rex. Recorded quickly in Piccadilly in March 1972, the album was a breathless collage of the band's many inspirations: Hollywood, fifties rock 'n' roll, krautrock. 'The concepts of collage and montage were totally invaluable, because my interests were so wide and diverse,' says Ferry. 'I was the one who was into Fred Astaire and Lotte Lenya and Sam Cooke and Leadbelly . . . hundreds of different musical things that were part of my background. There were so many ideas, it was like, Christ, let's get them all down before it goes away. Because you didn't know if you were ever going to *make* a second album! Nowadays you'd never do that, because you wouldn't want to confuse an audience. Even though the recording was poor, and the singing was terrible, it was also incredibly exciting.'

'the mind loses its bearings,' Simon Puxley wrote in elliptical sleeve notes that seemed to codify Roxy's glam aesthetic. *'what's the date again? (it's so dark in here). 1962? or twenty years on? is this a recording*

session or a cocktail party? { . . . } *musicians lie rigid-&-fluid in a manner-ist canvas of hard-edged black-leather glintings, red-satin slashes, smokey surrounding gloom* { . . . } *synthesized to whirls and whorls of hardrock sound . . . mixed/fixed/sifted/lifted to driving, high-flying chunks and vortices of pure electronic wow* { . . . } *Saturday nite at the Roxy the Mecca the Ritz – your fantasies realized . . .'*

From the hectic, 'Street Life'-style opening of 'Re-make/Re-model' – titled after Derek Boshier's 1962 painting 'Re-think, Re-entry' – through the stylized balladry of 'Chance Meeting' and 'Sea Breezes', to the twisted country rock of 'If There is Something', *Roxy Music* was a wild ride along Pop Art Boulevard, propelled by Mackay's squawking saxes and Eno's crazed synth oscillations. Rock 'n' roll, doo-wop, country and western, experimental doodling, campy crooning: the group had packed everything in to the nine songs. Couple that with Nick de Ville's cover – an anxiously lustful Ossie Clark model done up like a Victoria's Secret chocolate box – and it was clear this was something completely new in British pop.

All Roxy Music needed to make a splash was a hit single, which was why the considerably more radio-friendly 'Virginia Plain' was released in July 1972. I'll never forget hearing it the first time, lying in a tent in the Dordogne with the transistor clamped to my ear: it was like hearing a pop group from Neptune. On one level it was as basic and as catchy as a Slade record, but on another it wasn't pop music at all. Ferry, who was already twenty-seven, sounded more knowing than even Bowie. And when you finally saw him he looked like a spivvy Elvis, or Humphrey Bogart as Count Dracula. More startling still was Brian Eno: Rick Wakeman's kid sister, a vampy transsexual jester in black ostrich plumes and heavy purple eyeshadow.

'For me there was no sexual aspect to it,' says Eno. 'I was not gay, but I wanted to look great, and looking great meant dressing as a woman! Or at least as some kind of weird new hybrid of male and female. I was living with a woman named Carole McNicol, who was a sculptor and also a very good clothes-maker. I could think up ideas for clothes, and she would improve on the ideas and then actually make the clothes. I think we were really thinking in terms of sculpture – these were clothes that you could only really wear on stage, they were impossible to do anything normal in. When I went on to the stage, the only decision I can consciously remember making was this: what I do involves standing still on stage adjusting tiny little knobs, so it would make sense to have garments that magnify my movements. Hence the feathers and so on. So I wasn't doing very much, but it looked quite good.'

'When I met David Bowie in LA in 1972,' says Kim Fowley, 'I asked him what was going on in England and he went into a fifteen-minute description of Brian Eno and Roxy Music, with the emphasis on Eno's image. I got the impression that he was glad someone else with a brain was getting theatrical, so it wasn't just him. My memory is that he thought more of Brian Eno than he thought of any other glam person. I think he knew that Eno was doing more at the time than simply playing keyboards with Roxy Music – that there was some navigational, quasi-conceptual stuff going on.'

With 'Virginia Plain' at No. 4 in the charts, Roxy began playing live in earnest, and not always with felicitous results. Supporting Bowie at the Rainbow was one thing, but opening for Jethro Tull at Madison Square Garden was probably unwise. America, in any case, would never embrace Roxy Music. When even a writer like Lester Bangs could complain that the group's vitality was 'severely limited' by their 'artifice', it was clear that they would always be regarded with suspicion by glam-o-phobes.[2] Unlike Bowie, moreover, Roxy weren't interested in schmoozing at Max's Kansas City. 'I always felt I was on the outside of things,' says Ferry.

Back in London in February 1973, Roxy recorded the masterful *For Your Pleasure*. This was shimmering, sinister music that moved beyond pop art to create a futuristic sound of elegant gloom. The invigorating blast-off of 'Do the Strand' notwithstanding, most of *Pleasure* consisted of a solitary Ferry searching for feeling in a dehumanized universe: the universe of 'Beauty Queen', 'Editions of You', above all of the majestic 'In Every Dream Home a Heartache', that eerie hymn to a blow-

2 'Roxy Music's audience in America,' wrote Bangs (whose writing always betrayed an implicit machismo), 'is a bunch of young people who have picked up on their superficial stylistic mannerisms, reminiscent of the old Andy Warhol, and made them into the latest teenage fad. The girls all dress up in 1940s outfits and walk around acting bored while the boys mince around acting queer.'

up sex doll. 'For Your Pleasure' and 'Strictly Confidential' sounded like F. Scott Fitzgerald set to a soundtrack that was equal parts Leadbelly and Kraftwerk, brilliantly doctored and distorted by Eno.

'I remember Tony Palmer saying in the *Observer* that Roxy had pierced through to the dark horror at the centre of modern life,' says Simon Puxley. 'It was a very unusual way of appraising the band, but I think there was a certain truth in it. A lot of Bryan's songs were very dark and macabre, almost lethal in their effect.'[3]

Horror aside, Ferry was extremely proud of *For Your Pleasure*. 'I think I enjoyed making the second album more, because we were a little more in control, though still learning,' he says. 'I think Brian had more to do with the sound of the first two albums than anything, because that was his best role. He was more of a producer than a player.' Once again, Nick de Ville created a superb image for the album cover, with the hermaphroditic model Amanda Lear walking a panther against a backdrop of a neon-lit Las Vegas. The effect was one of sumptuous glam noir. On the inside sleeve Roxy looked fabulous, posing with unreal-looking guitars.

'*For your pleasure/In our present state/Part false, part true/Like anything/We present ourselves . . .*'

The tragedy was that Roxy mark one was doomed not to last: the group couldn't hold both Ferry and Eno. By July 1973 one of them had to go. 'I left because I had no choice,' remembers Eno. 'Bryan Ferry said, "I'm never going on stage with you again."' Did Ferry feel upstaged by the more charismatic Eno, or merely threatened by Eno's inquisitive, forever foraging intellect? 'There was definitely an ego clash,' says Eno, 'and this was sort of agitated by what happened around us rather than what happened between us. Because I was photogenic and wore clothes that were very demonstrative and looked good in magazines, I got a lot more attention than I deserved. I wasn't the writer, and I hadn't been there at the beginning. So there was that

---

3 In his book *Stargazer: Andy Warhol's World and His Films* (1973), Stephen Koch wrote that Warhol 'is an artist whose glamour is rooted in despair'; that Warhol 'proposes the momentary glow of a presence, an image – anyone's – if only they can leap out of the fade-out of inexistence into the presence of the star'. This seems as good a definition of what Roxy were doing as any I've read.

aspect of a typical young male competitiveness.'

'The reason it fell apart, I think, is that Bryan was doing all the work and Eno getting all the glory,' says David Enthoven. 'It was Eno who got to shag all the girls, and I think that drove Bryan completely bonkers. With Eno, it was the same thing as with Jagger – Jagger's appeal was that he moved like a woman. I mean, Eno was literally shagging non-stop; he was on for it all the time, like a fucking rabbit. I've never known anything like it.'

Further proof, then, that the more camp and androgynous you looked in 1973, the more girls fancied you. 'Women always seem to get on with gays, and I think it's slightly like that,' Eno offers as an explanation. 'It's the feeling that here is someone who is other but who is not threatening, who has surrendered their authority and their ability to command by strength. If you're gay or you're androgynous, you're not playing that usual male role of "I'm the tough one here." She knows that this guy isn't *playing the male*.

'I thought and still think that anything which erodes that easy distinction between male and female is a good thing. There was a whole kind of negative movement at the time saying either men were terrible or women were pathetic, and I thought, Why not just be neither of them? Why not side-step the whole argument by becoming something else, something in between? I still think that's a strong position. And of course it's a position that a lot of people have generally adopted – the New Man is a slightly feminized man, basically. A New Man is someone who doesn't think that looking after the children is humiliating, who doesn't think that showing emotions is unmasculine.'

And what did the cross-dressing Lothario do after getting the heaveho? Picked himself up and signed a solo deal with Island which brought the world those wondrous post-glam albums *Here Come the Warm Jets* (1973) and *Taking Tiger Mountain by Strategy* (1974). Eno was no singer, but he took the raw spirit of the first Roxy album and turned it into music of delighted whimsy, navigating a middle ground between glam – the prancing 'Baby's on Fire', the exultant 'Needle's in the Camel's Eye', the mutant Bo Diddley of 'Blank Frank' – and the more cerebral terrain of his work from *Another Green World* (1975) onwards. 'When I was working on *Warm Jets* and *Tiger Mountain*, I had pure energy going for me,' he says. 'I felt so thrilled to be out of Roxy, I never regretted it for one moment. I remember the day I left, running down the King's Road and sort of skipping and jumping. I thought, Now I can do anything. I guess I had this complete optimism that somehow or other I'd survive.'

'Eno's solo albums sold better than we thought they would,' says David Enthoven. 'We even took him out on the road with the Winkies, but he decided he didn't want to play live because he couldn't really pull it off. It was apparent that he was never going to be a great singer or frontman, and he couldn't just go on posturing and playing what were simplistic if very interesting songs. The audience that was coming to see him was quite serious, but he was playing fairly glib songs. So he rightly made the decision to get off stage, and I was very sad about it.'

Roxy Music, replacing Eno with the electric violinist Eddie Jobson, became a much slicker proposition. 'Once Eno left, it did change,' says Enthoven. 'A very strong voice had left, there's no doubt about it.' Even Bryan Ferry seems to concur with the view that a key ingredient was thenceforth missing from the recipe. 'I think I underestimated how big a help he'd been to me when we split up,' he says. 'To his credit, when I met Eno again for the first time ten years later he said *Stranded* was his favourite of the Roxy albums, but I sort of felt that *For Your Pleasure* was so good that we couldn't do anything in the same vein without repeating the same idea. I think I was wrong about that.'

By any other reckoning, *Stranded* (released in November 1973) was a superbly performed and produced record. 'Street Life' was a thrilling pop anthem, 'A Song for Europe' a majestic mini-symphony laced with Brechtian irony. The charged 'Mother of Pearl', starting at breakneck pace before slowing to a long hypnotic build-up, was Ferry alone again, searching for female perfection in a vapid world of deceptive surfaces. (*'With every goddess a letdown, every idol a breakdown/It gets you down . . .'*) And the exquisite finale, 'Sunset' – just Ferry at the piano and an acoustic bass – could almost have been an elegy for the glam era that was now starting to fade.

'Sunset, end of my dreams . . . my decline . . .'

By now Ferry had already plotted a course for himself as a solo star, taking his *faux*-matinée-idol image to its logical conclusion on the

1973 covers album *These Foolish Things*. (Like Bowie with *Pin-Ups*, Ferry was old enough to plug into the same nostalgia – the same desire to recast the golden oldies of the fifties and sixties – that produced John Lennon's *Rock and Roll* and The Band's *Moondog Matinée*.) Some of the slickness, he concedes, had rubbed off on Roxy. 'The musicality of *Foolish Things* had seeped over into *Stranded*,' says Ferry. 'That plus the fact that without Eno there was less opportunity to monkey around with the sound. But some of the songs on *Stranded* were just as good. It was better played, and we had a proper producer for the first time.'

By 1974 Roxy had all but abandoned glam as a mode of presentation. From *Country Life* onwards, Ferry would opt for elegance, or mere costumery: the Zorro look, the GI uniforms. In the end he turned out to be less kinky and subversive than we'd all thought. 'I remember that there was this great jacket of Antony's with black sequins and a green chevron that I wore on *Top of the Pops*,' he says. 'But shortly after that you saw Gary Glitter wearing the same kind of things, and that's where the tuxedo came in. By that time we'd made some sort of mark, and people knew who we were, and we felt we didn't have to look so outrageous any more.'

Roxy Music had become just another rock band.

all dressed up
(with somewhere to go)

'Our function really is to relieve adolescents of their ills, of all the mental cruelty that's been bestowed on them . . .'

David Johansen

The sweet young things – and the male predators – of Rodney Bingenheimer's English Disco

When David Bowie met Iggy Pop at Max's in September 1971, the live music scene in Manhattan was all but dead. New York had always been inhospitable to bands, but the emphasis now was purely on hanging out, with the occasional foray on to small dance floors. Too jaded to seek out the city's new Velvet Undergrounds, the downtown scenesters – and uptown slummers – simply wanted to ogle and bitch about each other.

The snobbish attitude to local live music was exemplified by the reaction to Mickey Ruskin's decision to book bands in the upstairs room at Max's. 'The really fun period ended as soon as they started bringing the bands in, because it brought in a lot of riff-raff,' said Danny Fields, publicist for Elektra Records. 'To the patrons of the first era of Max's, rock music interfered with and interrupted the flow of life at Max's Kansas City. Sure, there was a discotheque upstairs with Wayne County spinning, but that was fine with everyone because it didn't attract the outer-borough scum.' Even the nascent New York Dolls failed to endear themselves to the in-crowd. 'We were never really that welcomed by the Candy Darlings and Jackie Curtises,' said Syl Sylvain. 'They didn't really see the potential in the new wave of kids coming in.'

'When I went to MacDougal Street as a teenager, there were so many bands,' says David Johansen. 'Then all of a sudden there was no place to play, whether because of a police crackdown or not I don't know. It just went through this very fallow period. It had to do with these really Draconian cabaret laws they'd had since the twenties. When we started with the Dolls there was no scene. I used to hang around at Max's and they would have bands there upstairs, but that was it. The Velvets played there for, like, a summer – and it was horrible! Or they would have Waylon Jennings or Billy Joe Shaver. But there wasn't any rock 'n' roll. Because what was rock 'n' roll? You were either playing at some big joint like the Fillmore, or you were going in a bus from town to town.'

It was another club which provided the seedbed for a new scene – a scene made up, significantly, of the 'outer-borough' kids so despised by the Max's clientele. Nobody's, on Bleecker Street, was where kids like Johnny Genzale (a.k.a. Johnny Volume, a.k.a. Johnny Thunders) would meet and parade their new glam togs. 'They used to get their clothes at Granny Takes a Trip, and they'd have these velvet suits and the Rod Stewart rooster haircuts,' recalls Johansen. 'And Nobody's was their kind of pick-up bar. These were people who had jobs essentially, and then at night they'd be peacocks. I used to go there at night and check it out, because there were a lot of beautiful girls there. And John used to hang around there, coz he was from Queens, and he was a mover and shaker in the Queens mod scene. Plus he'd been to England, which was like being an astronaut.'

According to the Dolls' second drummer, Jerry Nolan, it was Genzale's girlfriend Janis who turned him on to glam. 'He was wearing high heels, and you remember that teased-hair, Rod Stewart look? Johnny's was like that, but even more dimensionalized and exaggerated, teased all the way up like in a crown. He would have a platinum-blond streak down the back . . . a girl's blouse on, and on top of that a sparkling girl's vest. And then maybe a cowboy scarf. Mixing in cowboy stuff with glamorous forties girl stuff was something the Dolls liked to do. And he wore make-up, which really set him off.'

Johansen, in his own words, was 'a little rangier' and harder up than Genzale. He also had a more arty agenda than the peacocks of Nobody's, having appeared in Ridiculous Theatrical Company productions like *Whores of Babylon*, and even in a couple of porn movies. He might have grown up on Staten Island, but by the age of sixteen he was working after school in a clothing store in St Mark's Place, the epicentre of downtown cool.

'This was the dawn of feminism and gay politics,' he says. 'All this stuff was coming through me – all this radical thought, not just about overthrowing the government but about what sexuality was, what maleness was and what femaleness was. All of it was erupting at the time. There were certain guys, either of a hetero- or homo- or bisexual persuasion, who were kinda morphing into this androgyny thing. I mean, it was just happening on the street, it wasn't like there were clubs or anything. Jackie Curtis was one of the people who took it to the street. Jackie wanted to be an Andy Warhol star, but basically the scene was on the street, like at St Mark's and 2nd Street. There were all these elements of the same social change. And a lot of acid going on, which certainly made it possible to go with the thing and not ever stop to think, "Is this insane?" because it just seemed totally normal.'

When Johansen first connected with guitarist Thunders, drummer Billy Murcia and bassist Arthur Harold Kane in January 1972, he knew he'd found the vehicle he'd been searching for: a band that would combine R&B raunch with low-rent, flea-market glamour. 'It wasn't like we were wearing fringed jackets and we decided to look like this,' says Johansen. 'We already looked like that. We'd seen the Stones wearing make-up, we'd seen the Pretty Things, the Flamin' Groovies – that was the basis of the look. When I met these guys it was like, yeah, this is what I wanna do. The Stones were definitely the best thing going. The music was R&B-based rock 'n' roll. I was not an aficionado of white music really. If white guys were playing black music, then it was OK. Everybody in the Dolls had their different idols. Billy loved Marc Bolan, he thought that was where it was at. I thought that if we could be as popular as the Velvet Underground we'd have it made. Which is certainly setting your sights really low!'

Replacing rhythm guitarist Rick Rivets with Syl Sylvain, the band began rehearsing in a bicycle shop on the Upper West Side, blasting out covers like Archie Bell and the Drells' '(There's Gonna be a) Showdown' and Sonny Boy Williamson's 'Don't Start Me Talkin'' till the sun came up. 'John said, we're gonna call this band the Dolls,' says Johansen. 'And like a jerk I made it the New York Dolls. Which really was stupid, because people hate New York!' Stupid or not, the Dolls looked and sounded fabulous: the chemistry was pure Stones/Faces, with Johansen and Thunders duplicating the Jagger/Richards, Stewart/Wood dynamic, while sound was a trashy amalgam of R&B, girl-group pop and garage-band fuzz. Johansen himself was one of the great frontmen, a debauched cupidon who looked like Peter Noone crossed with the Malcolm McDowell of *A Clockwork Orange*.

To a fan like Jerry Nolan, who would soon be drumming in Wayne County's band Queen Elizabeth, the Dolls were simply bringing back the three-minute song in an era of ten-minute drum solos. After a couple of scuzzy midtown gigs in the early spring of 1972, Johansen got word from Max's regular (and Warhol veteran) Eric Emerson that there was a new place to play downtown. Emerson had formed his own band, the Magic Tramps, and was holding down a regular night at the Mercer Arts Center, a theatre arts complex which had been renovated in a style that coupled *Clockwork Orange* decor with Victorian chandeliers. 'Eric was out of his mind, but he was a great guy,' says Johansen. 'He had a thing going in the video room, the Kitchen, where Nam June Paik would put on his videos of John Giorno taking a nap or whatever, and he said, "Why don't you come in and play with *me?*" So we went down and opened for him, and Al Lewis – who booked the place and was this old-time showbiz guy with a suit and toupee – comes running up to me and says, "Play again! Play again!" After the show he said he wanted to give us our own room, on Tuesdays at midnight.'

The room, fittingly enough, was called the Oscar Wilde Room, and it was here, in April 1972, that the New York Dolls' Tuesday night residency became the stuff of Manhattan legend. 'It was almost Felliniesque, with these people on bleachers surrounding the band, and the band playing in the middle of this crowd,' recalls photographer Bob Gruen. 'It was sort of hard to tell who was in the band and who wasn't. Everybody was drunk or stoned on quaaludes, reds, cocaine – the chaos level was pretty high, and it was the most exciting thing I'd ever seen.' Suddenly a whole scene began to coalesce around the Dolls, with nubile teenage girls swarming in from the suburbs to be part of the new urban satyricon. 'The Dolls have been getting a lot of people in New York off their decadent asses and making them dance,' noted Ed McCormack in *Interview*. Johansen himself saw the band simply as a reflection of its audience: 'They're hip, sophisticated little New York kids, [and] I just watch them and become them.'

'If you were lucky enough to catch one of the Dolls' brilliant gigs, it was indescribable,' says Bebe Buell, who dragged her sceptical boyfriend, Todd Rundgren, along one Tuesday night. 'I think that everybody just needed to replace the Velvet Underground, as far as having a hometown band. Everybody was very festively dressed and having sex with each other. There were always extracurricular sexual activities going on, and there were a lot of loft gatherings, people trying to recreate the Factory feel. Sometimes there'd be parties, and the Dolls would start playing, or the Magic Tramps would start playing. Eric was astounding. He could leap through the air like Rudolf Nureyev. He would wear Iggy Pop costumes but add sparkles and glitter to his costumes. Iggy could contort, but Eric could fly through the air like a fucking bird.'

Other acts who emerged from the woodwork to play at the Mercer included Teenage Lust, the Miamis, the Harlots of 42nd Street, Ruby and the Rednecks, and even the notorious Suicide, whose severe and minimal sound, part Velvets and part Stooges, generally had the effect of clearing any room they played in.[1] 'All of a sudden there was a place to play,' says David Johansen. 'And when you have a venue or two, people start thinking, Hey, we'll make a band. I loved the Harlots of 42nd Street: they were just these really working-class guys with hairy arms, but they wanted to be like us. They'd come in with these ripped fishnets and broken heels. We were raunchy but they were worse – they were so ill-suited to androgyny, and I just loved them for that reason. They had the vocabulary of orang-utans, but they were really sweet.'

The most outrageous of all the Mercer bands was Wayne County's Queen Elizabeth, whose Ridiculous Theater-inspired act involved not only glitter and platforms but dildos and fake dogshit – like *Pink Flamingos* set to rock 'n' roll. 'While these groups and their fans on this burgeoning scene profess to be parodying or "camping" on various sexual styles,' observed *Crawdaddy*, 'it is difficult to say where affectation ends and reality begins.' Which was precisely what had always distinguished the Iggy Pops from the Alice Coopers.

It's funny to think now how completely out of kilter New York was with the rest of America in 1972. Today MTV would be beaming the Dolls into every small-town living room in the country, but back then the Mercer scene was deemed to be so extreme and marginal that no record company dared to sign them. 'Andy [Warhol] had a very commercial streak, but most of the bands I saw playing didn't expect to get anywhere,' says Bob Gruen. 'This wasn't about becoming famous, it was about getting a few girls from Brooklyn or Queens to like you.

1 Although Suicide were not a glam act *per se*, when *Melody Maker*'s Roy Hollingworth saw them play the Mercer in October 1972 he noted that singer Alan Vega's face was 'covered in glitter'.

72

There was no expectation of acceptance. It was just sort of fun. You never expected to get on the radio; I mean, *Lou Reed* didn't get on the radio. It was so small and underground, it was beyond anybody's dreams that it would ever mean anything.'

'Radio stations in mainstream America would not *touch* this stuff,' said Danny Fields. 'It's a very conservative industry: the promoters were conservative, the radio stations were and are conservative. Sexual ambiguity was more acceptable in England, where there's always been this camp tradition. In America it was all horrifying, deep-seated righteousness and biblical homophobia. It was an atrocious sensibility that's rampant in America to this day, and people rebelled against it. But there was no way to break through on musical merit once you put on lipstick.'

What made the Dolls stand apart from the other Mercer bands – what, ultimately, *did* get them signed – was that their songs were genuinely great. To the sublime, searing riffs of Thunders and Sylvain, Johansen would write trenchant vignettes of New York flotsam and jetsam like 'Trash', 'Bad Girl' and 'Personality Crisis'. 'Rimbaud would write about the monstrous city and the effects it would have on the species,' he noted in a publicity blurb. 'And here it is in 1973 and everything is very fast moving and I try to understand how people feel about it, how they relate to the environment.'

'The Dolls were very special in that they really did have a deeper perception of who they were,' says Bob Gruen. 'They were basically very R&B-oriented, but the songs that they wrote were really brilliant, politically and socially. It was about cultural politics.' Even the snooty Max's crowd – titillated by the possibility that these glam boys might actually be gay – was won over by the group's sheer panache and wit. 'The Dolls created a huge scene, and it became extremely fashionable to go see them,' said Leee Black Childers. 'It was an actual participatory thing. Everybody in the audience was just as outlandish as the Dolls were. There was Wayne County, the Harlots, Sylvia Miles, Don Johnson, Patti D'Arbanville, all that kind of gang. And then of course David Bowie and Lou Reed, watching and learning.'

Reed merely wheezed that the Dolls were 'very cute', but the more generous Bowie acknowledged David Johansen as an equal, someone who, as he later put it, 'had the stance of it being some kind of breakdown between high and low art'. (Thunders, he said, was 'into the Keith Richards archetype', but Johansen 'was part of a Warhol crowd and knew exactly what he was doing'.) Not long after Bowie saw them at the Mercer in October 1972 – an experience which supposedly inspired *Aladdin Sane*'s 'Watch That Man' – the Dolls actually travelled to England to play a handful of dates, including one supporting the Faces at Wembley's Empire Pool. The British press lapped up this band which hadn't even secured a record deal, and the Dolls took full advantage of the hype. 'People were driving us around in Daimlers,' chuckles Johansen. 'We were from the street and people were treating us like royalty. Lord Montagu held a party for us at Beaulieu! I had never been in a house like that. Meanwhile we're in a hotel, three guys to a room.'

Unfortunately, tragedy struck in London when, on 6 November, Billy Murcia overdosed on alcohol and Mandrax and died. But this only had the effect of making the Dolls more alluring than they already were: when Jerry Nolan played his first show with the band six weeks later, more people were trying to cram themselves into the Mercer than ever. Now, moreover, the record companies were finally paying some attention. 'When we moved into the big room at the Mercer, all the big guys came to see us on the same night,' says Johansen. 'The managers figured, Let's get a bidding frenzy for this band. But I think they were all really frightened of us, they thought we were just too out there. And when it came time to get a producer, nobody would produce us. Nobody wanted to be in a room with us.'

The one exception was Todd Rundgren, who had been introduced to the Dolls by Bebe Buell. When Paul Nelson of Mercury Records finally put his neck on the line and signed the group, Rundgren – one of the hottest producers in America at that point – committed himself to producing their first album. 'I knew Todd from Max's,' says Johansen, 'and he knew I wasn't gonna bite his head off. We were lucky to get him.'[2]

2 Rundgren himself was a kind of missing link between sixties hippie chic and seventies glam overkill. His late-sixties band the Nazz were proto-dandies who blew much of their advance on buying clothes from Granny Takes a Trip, and by the early seventies he was sporting make-up and wild multicoloured hair. In November 1973 his bizarre get-up on the rock show *Midnight Special* – which the Dolls also famously

The New York Dolls took exactly a week to record, and no one seems to remember the sessions too clearly. 'It's like a blackout – a minute here, a minute there,' says Johansen. 'We had to hurry up and finish it because we had a gig in Buffalo or something. In the end Todd got so fed up with everyone saying, "Turn me up," that he just turned *everybody* up. And that's probably how it was produced. The other guys said, "Todd fucked up the record," but that's bullshit. God bless him, we were lucky to have someone who could get the band to play all at once.'

'There were lots of drugs and lots of insanity,' says Bebe Buell. 'It was difficult to find any order. I was surprised the record even got completed, to be honest. It almost killed Todd. I went to visit one time, and I thought he was gonna have a nervous breakdown. Everybody was bouncing off the walls, and shouting that they should be louder and louder. Johnny Thunders was going, "Turn the guitars up!" And I was sort of agreeing with him. I don't think Todd was given a proper chance to pull that album together. I still think it's a classic – right up there with *Raw Power* and *Never Mind the Bollocks*. It's a milestone, a monumental record. I got very pissed off when Johnny Thunders put the record down. I mean, what were they expecting? I think it's coherent. You can hear how intelligent the lyrics are, how clever and unique their style is.'

As with *Raw Power*, the controversy over the supposedly 'thin' sound seems unwarranted now. However you hear it, it's still an impossibly exciting record, full of squalling guitars, storming riffs and wickedly

played – almost derailed his career. 'At that point Todd was into this sort of existential sort of paint-me, use-me-as-a-piece-of-art kick, and he let his gay make-up artist Nicky Nichols do whatever he wanted,' says Paul Fishkin, then of Bearsville Records. 'He goes on *Midnight Special* doing this beautiful loping smash-hit ballad ['Hello, It's Me'], and Nicky has made him up with wings and painted his eyes as multicoloured teardrops. The world is watching, and this is the Todd they see – a fucking drag queen.' Bebe Buell called it 'the Man-Eating Peacock outfit': 'You look back now and it was no nuttier than Peter Gabriel dressed as a sunflower, but Nicky was not only highly creative and highly gay but stoned out of his mind with unlimited access to feathers! It wasn't sabotage; I think Todd thought everyone would like it. We were all so upset.' For more on Rundgren, see the author's 'Go Ahead, Ignore Me!', *Mojo*, February 1998.

camp asides that piss all over . . . well, *Goat's Head Soup*, for a start. And that was nothing compared to the cover, a *pièce de résistance* stage-managed by the designer Betsy Johnson and her friends Bunky and Nini. Never have I forgotten my first sight of this masterpiece lying on the counter at Virgin Records off Sloane Square: in an era ruled by hirsute dudes like the Allman Brothers, who or what *was* this vampy quintet of transsexual pretty boys?

'At the time I was really into the androgyny thing,' says Johansen. 'I really thought that that was where it was at – that there should be no difference. I later came to believe that women should be women and men should be men, but at that time – I don't wanna make us sound like saints of androgyny or anything, because we were pretty rough around the edges and definitely exploiting it for all it was worth – it was kind of noble. This was beyond feminism.'

Watching the Dolls play the Mercer in February 1973 – on a Valentine's Day bill with the Magic Tramps, Queen Elizabeth et al. – the English writer Miles was astonished by the spectacle of 'a new wave of New York groups who've picked up on Bolan, Slade, Elton and Bowie in a big way and combined them with such historical figures as the Fugs, the early Mothers and Lou Reed', and observed that 'LA soft-rock has been stomped on by glittering, lurid, day-glo platform shoes'. London could boast nothing like Wayne County, resplendent in a huge green-and-pink Afro wig, penetrating a strap-on plastic vagina as he screeched 'It Takes a Man Like Me to Fuck a Woman Like Me'.[3] The audience itself was 'a welter of day-glo, Lurex, tinsel, glitter dust on flesh and clothes, studs, satin, silk, and leather, lurid reds, pink angora tops, green boas, totally transparent blouses and multicoloured platforms'. The effect, Miles concluded, was 'quite sinister after London, which still tends more towards the warmth and friendliness of lace and velvet'.

'Our glam scene had more punk-rock resonance in it than the English scene,' says Bebe Buell. 'It was a marriage of punk and glitter,

3 County was actually signed to MainMan, with Tony DeFries touting him to record companies as a cross between Bette Midler and Iggy Pop. Not surprisingly, the record companies failed to take the bait.

whereas in Britain it was either punk *or* glitter. You see, the street life of Manhattan *was* the wild side. The only thing you could compare it to was pre-war Berlin. There was a whole other thing going on here, too, and that was the whole drug thing. Some bad drugs, heroin, needles. When I looked up at the Empire State Building, I thought, Now I know why everyone comes to New York to be a junkie.'

Drugs would soon bring about the downfall of the New York Dolls, but not before they had dragged their trash-aesthetic mission across the length and breadth of America. 'We were popular in Florida, Atlanta, Detroit, Cleveland and Chicago,' says Johansen. 'The rust belt was big for us for some reason. In Detroit they were real tough but they'd wear boas and lipstick. And the chicks had black eyes.'

Nothing could quite have prepared the Dolls for Los Angeles, where they were greeted by a veritable panoply of teenage female flesh as they checked in to the notorious Continental Hyatt 'Riot House', on Sunset Boulevard.

If LA would seem to have been a natural place for glam to take root – its celluloid heroes had inspired at least half the imagery for glam rock – it was none the less still dominated by the mewling canyon-rock sound of Crosby, Stills, Nash and their kind. Indeed, Rodney Bingenheimer, the so-called 'Mayor of Sunset Strip' in its mid-sixties heyday, was so bored by LA in 1971 that he went to live in London. He says that he 'had had enough of women with hair on their legs'.

Working as a press officer for Mercury Records, then David Bowie's US label, Bingenheimer sat in on several sessions for *Hunky Dory*. He also went with his girlfriend, Melanie McDonald – later the companion of Tony DeFries – to a club in Ealing called the Cellar. 'They were playing all these amazing records like T. Rex and the Sweet,' he remembers. 'And I always kept that in the back of my mind, and I went and told David about it, and he said, "Yeah, you should do a club like that in LA."'

Bingenheimer had first met Bowie when the singer visited California in January 1971. He'd thrown Bowie a huge party at a house belonging to Warhol star Ultra Violet, and had arranged for him to stay with the producer and manager Tom Ayres in the Hollywood Hills. What struck him most was that, despite his exaggeratedly feminine appearance – one which got them thrown out of a Hollywood restaurant – Bowie was 'grabbing girls left and right . . . picking up girls hitchhiking in the street'.

Eighteen months later, when Bowie came to LA to play the Santa Monica Civic on 20 October 1972, Bingenheimer and Ayres opened the E Club on Sunset Boulevard. Bowie's entrance that night, attired in full Ziggy regalia, signalled the birth of glam in Hollywood. 'Alone in LA, Rodney seemed like myself, an island of Anglo "nowness",' Bowie told *Details*. 'He even knew British singles and bands that *I* wasn't aware of. Rodney single-handedly cut a path through the treacle of the sixties, allowing all us "avants" to parade our sounds of tomorrow dressed in our clothes of derision.'

When the club moved eastwards to 7561 Sunset three months later, Rodney became the crown prince of the Hollywood glam scene. And just as foxy nymphets were drawn to the Mercer Arts Center, so the sweet things of southern California flocked to this Anglophile oasis, renamed Rodney Bingenheimer's English Disco for its 15 December opening. 'Glam leapfrogged to LA via the Mercer Arts Center,' says Rodney's crony Kim Fowley. 'I had just come from London, and I was shocked to find the scene I'd seen in England replicated. Rodney had all the music. The English Disco was a more public-toilet version of the E Club. The new location gave it the teenage stench it needed. Everybody had great hair and great make-up, and there were Lolita girls everywhere. People worked at it.'

While Bingenheimer and Fowley held court at the English Disco, all of Hollywood came to gawp at the black-lipsticked, Quaalude-gobbling, platform-booted groupies – outrageous vixens like Sable Starr, Lori Lightning, Coral Shields and 'Gas Chamber' Nancy. 'The groupies were usually girls who did not have fathers, lived in disenfranchised homes and had mothers who worked,' says Fowley. 'They came for feminine men who weren't queer. Of course, anyone who had Bowie-esque qualities automatically got lucky.'

'LA took the glitter thing to the extreme,' says Bebe Buell. 'It really took with the girls out there. Whereas in New York the word "groupie" was an insult, in LA it was considered an honour. When I met Sable and

Lori, they introduced themselves to me as the world's greatest groupies. Girls like Sable and Lori didn't have to lift a finger to be desirable. Miss Pamela [Des Barres] did not take well to the surge of the new young girls. She was still living in that sixties glamorous rich-hippie thing, and when the new breed of kid came along, younger and bolder and less intimidated by other people's opinions, it was all very threatening to her.'

Miss Pamela, who married Michael Des Barres of glam hard-rock band Silverhead – a fixture of the LA scene after their splendidly titled second album *16 and Savaged* – says that 'as much as I love Rodney, the English Disco just wasn't the same thing as we'd had in 1965 – there was a little desperation, almost trying to re-create what had been there on the Strip eight years before'. For Pamela, moreover, 'there was such backstabbing in the groupie scene, whereas in the sixties we were all *for* each other, and that was more important than any one guy'.

The music at Rodney's disco was all English, and mostly records. 'People didn't really wanna hear bands,' says Bingenheimer. 'They liked the records. It was a rock disco. There was a certain dance where you'd lean down and kinda wiggle your shoulders.' (No surprise, given how hard it was to dance in six-inch platform heels.) 'Rodney played the music you couldn't hear anywhere else,' remembered Joan Jett. 'Gary Glitter, Slade, Sweet, T. Rex, and a lot of obscure stuff you never heard on the radio. Glam rock was such a unique sound, melodic, but with lots of emphasis on the drums and loud guitars and those big chanting choruses.'[4] Particularly favoured was what Bingenheimer himself calls 'the mechanical stomp' of the great Chinn and Chapman singles. While 'Ballroom Blitz' blasted out across the dance floor and the dancers watched themselves in the wall-to-wall mirrors, Bingenheimer projected slides of pictures he'd taken during tapings of *Top of the Pops* in London. The beer on tap was Watney's.[5]

When actual Englishmen came to Rodney's, they were astonished at

4 Jett herself was particularly smitten with Suzi Quatro, a gay icon before her time. When a poster of Quatro in a black leather bikini was swiped from the English Disco, the culprit turned out to have been the pubescent Jett.
5 Although the club was primarily a disco, with the emphasis on records, there was briefly a kind of house band at Rodney's called Zolar-X. 'They were the first LA glam-rock band,' says Kim Fowley. 'They used the *Clockwork Orange* look, and they

the bacchanalian brazenness of the scene. 'The groupies were certainly pretty obvious,' recalled Steve Priest of the Sweet. 'They were just little girls who wore red sequins – and that's about all. And they weren't timid. They all acted like Mae West.' Some Englishmen were horrified. 'The really famous groupies were extremely tough and unpleasant,' recalls the writer Nick Kent. 'These conniving, loveless little girls really affected my whole concept of femininity for a while. Talk to the bass player from the Sweet and he would probably say those were the best months of his life. But to someone with a bit of taste, who wasn't just hopelessly addicted to pussy, it was pretty sordid. It was a period when, if you were skinny and English and dressed like some horrible Biba girl, you could have anything you wanted.'

The New York Dolls could have attested that you didn't even have to be English. 'The Dolls were real important,' says Rodney Bingenheimer, 'because they were guys dressed in high heels and leather and all that shit. It was like they were from England, except they were from New York.' When the Dolls played LA, the groupies went into overdrive: Sable Starr even forsook her wanton ways and became Johnny Thunders's old lady – if you could be an old lady at fifteen. 'There was this wild scene out there just waiting for us,' says David Johansen. 'It was like kids in the candy store and the owner was asleep. I don't think I slept for a week.'[6]

Another presence on the English Disco scene was Iggy Pop, who had become a forlorn figure in the glam world. Unceremoniously dropped

had a great frontman.' A press release from the time lists the band members as Eon Flash, Zanny Zantovian, Wiggy Ygarist and Steve Ygarr, while their songs included 'Mirrors', 'Jet Star', 'Space Age Love' and 'Test Tube Babies'. Were they any good? We may never know, although Rodney Bingenheimer has some of their demo tapes.

6 Bob Gruen's half-hour Dolls documentary *Looking for a Kiss* contains some riveting footage of the band in LA, including a scene where David Johansen dances to David Bowie's version of 'Waiting for the Man' at the English Disco. It's particularly poignant watching Johnny Thunders, a spunky young blade with Sable Starr dripping off his arm. Being a good Italian-American boy, of course, he wasn't too happy about sharing her with other rock stars. Sable even came back to New York with him, but – according to David Johansen's girlfriend, Cyrinda Foxe – couldn't cut it in Manhattan. 'After I was with Johnny,' she said rather pathetically, 'I just wasn't Sable Starr any more.'

by MainMan, he had fallen back into bad old ways and was often to be seen lurking around Rodney's. 'Iggy would come to the club wearing long dresses and flashing people and getting up in the DJ booth,' recalls Bingenheimer. Kid Congo, sometime guitarist with the Cramps and the Gun Club, remembers 'Iggy in the street outside the Disco, pulling his dress up and exposing himself, and Rodney crying because he thought he was going to be arrested . . .'

'Iggy was going out with Sable Starr's sister, Coral Shields,' says Nick Kent. 'He tried to stop using heroin and then got into an even worse state with Quaaludes and other tranquillizers. He was very quickly regarded as a loser, mainly because he wasn't English. My most abiding memory is of him standing at the English Disco in his *Raw Power* clothes, stoned, looking at himself in the mirrored walls for hours on end. It was pretty sad.'

Iggy's abjection none the less produced some of his most frighteningly intense performances: at Max's Kansas City in July 1972 and LA's Whisky a Go Go in September 1973, the Popster was at his self-destructive greatest, a silver-haired crazyman taking a death trip to the edge of oblivion. 'To me, the best band of that era, the band that blew everyone away, was the Stooges,' says Bebe Buell, on whose account Iggy lacerated his chest during the band's stand at Max's. Many of the songs Iggy and guitarist James Williamson wrote at this period – outbursts of splenetic misogyny like 'Rich Bitch' and 'She-Creatures of the Hollywood Hills' – were about the whole underworld of the English Disco. 'The youth thing is particularly pounded into you in America,' Iggy told me in 1986. 'When I was living in LA in very reduced circumstances during that period, I would meet these horrible little girls there who were fifteen and were fearing becoming nineteen. And that's not healthy, that's sick.'

By 1974, Iggy had turned Stooges gigs into grotesquely brilliant freakshows where anything could happen – and which usually wound up in bloody chaos. (The classic *Metallic KO*, recorded in his home town of Detroit in February of that year, remains a priceless document of this demented phase.) 'I still remember why I did those things and I still remember doing them *very clearly*,' he says. 'I remember the actions more than their consequences, saying what I said and doing what I did and all that. And I'm proud of it in a real funny and silly way, having been this real kind of picaresque figure. I still get a laugh out of *Metallic KO.*'

Iggy's day would come again, of course. For just around the corner, beyond the valley of the New York Dolls, lay punk rock.

beyond the valley of the dolls

'You won't fool the children of the revolution . . .'
Marc Bolan

The Dolls at Biba, November 1973: Syl Sylvian, David Johansen, Johnny Thunders

England, November 1973: T. Rex are in decline, with the dire 'Truck On (Tyke)' failing even to make the Top Ten and the sub-Ziggy *Zinc Alloy and the Hidden Riders of Tomorrow* lined up for release in early 1974. David Bowie himself has forsaken the future for the past with the sixties covers album *Pin-Ups*, and Lou Reed has followed up *Transformer* with the dark gloomfest *Berlin*, about a crumbling relationship between two speed freaks.[1]

The glitter-pop craze shows no signs of abating: 1973 began with Sweet's 'Blockbuster!' at No. 1 and will finish with Slade's 'Merry Xmas Everybody' in the same position. Providing the perfect teen counter-point to the solemn pomp of Pink Floyd's *Dark Side of the Moon* and the trippy country rock of the Grateful Dead, the RAK and Bell Records stables are still notching up big hits: the Sweet with 'Hell Raiser' and 'Ballroom Blitz', Slade with 'Cum On Feel the Noize' and 'Skweeze Me Pleeze Me', Gary Glitter with 'I'm the Leader of the Gang (I Am)' and 'I Love You Love Me Love'. 'Glam rock is dead,' mutters Marc Bolan. 'It was a great thing, but now you have your Sweet, your Chicory Tip, your Gary Glitter . . . what those guys are doing is circus and comedy.'

By now, the leading lights of *Top of the Pops* schlock have been joined by a slew of canny opportunists, or by simple spin-offs like Gary Glitter's Glitter Band. As Glitter himself did, tame sixties rocker Shane Fenton undergoes the tackiest of metamorphoses and emerges as Alvin Stardust, a glam Gene Vincent devoid of any real menace or sensuality. When this karaoke ghoul performs the hideous 'My Coo Ca Choo' on *Top of the Pops*, he doesn't even have a glam band behind him, just a bunch of bearded pub rockers whose only concession to glitter is that

1 Using the then divided city as a metaphor for Jim and Caroline's fracturing rela-tionship, *Berlin* invoked a Brechtian netherworld but stripped it of the Isherwoodian kinkiness that permeates Bowie's 'Time', Roxy Music's 'Bitter-Sweet' and other *Cabaret*-influenced glam songs. (Note that Bowie later recorded Brecht and Weill's 'Alabama Song', which the Doors had cut on their 1967 debut.) The album is emblematic of glam's dark undertow – of the price paid for the hedonism of the Max's/Rodney's scenes. Death is suddenly in the air. Max's mainstay Andrea Feldman kills herself. Reed's own wife, Betty, attempts suicide (inspiring *Berlin*'s 'The Kids' in the process). 'There is a beauty that arises not from happiness but from wretchedness, an efflorescence of decay,' writes Timothy Ferris of the album in *Rolling Stone*. Both David Bowie and Iggy Pop will move to Berlin after the glam era has ended.

they wear T-shirts with 'Alvin Stardust' written on them.[2]

Meanwhile, the Move's Roy Wood launches Wizzard and turns himself into a delinquent harlequin, backed by a group of gorilla-suited guitarists and teddy-boy saxophonists. With hits like 'See My Baby Jive' and 'Angel Fingers', Wizzard represent the intersection of glam with the nostalgia for fifties rock 'n' roll and sixties Spectorpop. The same might be said for the idiotic teddy-boy pop of Mud, fronted by a ghastly pub Elvis in brothel creepers – 'mutton dressed up as glam,' as Nicky Chinn, the architect of Mud's undeniably infectious 'Tiger Feet', describes bespectacled singer Les Gray. (Even here there is genuine androgyny at work, with guitarist Rob Davis dolled up in pink chiffon pantaloons and clusters of baubles pinned to his ears.)

One of the big glam successes of the year is Elton John, whose double album *Goodbye Yellow Brick Road* not only features 'Bennie and the Jets' (yet another Ziggy-esque creation, boasting a female singer in 'electric boots and mohair suit'), but boasts a cover illustration of John in spangly red platforms. Leaving behind the Americana of his earlier albums, *Yellow Brick Road* shows John aligning himself with glam while continuing to root himself in the hallowed craft of the singing-songwriting 'piano man'. Pretty soon, John's wardrobe will eclipse anything Bowie or Bolan or Roxy has worn. Indeed, John is so smitten with glam that – in an attempt to sign Iggy Pop to his Rocket record label – he takes the stage in a gorilla suit during a Stooges gig in Atlanta. Unfortunately, the plan backfires when a wasted Iggy mistakes John for a real gorilla and freaks.

In London, a mood of languorous decadence has descended on the pop scene, centred on the ultra-hip Kensington department store Biba. 'Right then and there, it felt as if our party would just go on getting bigger, richer, sweeter and wilder for ever,' Angie Bowie would write of life in and around Chelsea. 'It may have been Nero fiddling, but he was playing a hell of a tune.' With its Art Deco Hollywood designs and

2 Did Hoagy Carmichael know what he'd started when he wrote 'Stardust'? Could the Legendary Stardust Cowboy have guessed how ubiquitous the word would become after David Bowie appropriated it for the cyber-hybrid that was Ziggy Stardust? By the time the David Essex film *Stardust* was released in 1974, the word had become a kind of code term for glam.

transsexual fashions, Biba is where the capital's beautiful people converge – and where glam bands periodically perform in the top-floor Rainbow Room.

'The wonderful thing about Biba was that they were never concerned about making money,' says photographer Mick Rock. 'It was one of the first stores where they actively encouraged you to hang out, and if you didn't buy anything no one was gonna bother you. They had big parties on the roof garden or in the Rainbow Room, and you'd see everybody there: Justin de Villeneuve, Michael Roberts, Janet Street-Porter, Amanda Lear, Freddi Buretti, Molly Parkin, Andrew Logan, Derek Jarman. The three big glam designers were Bill Gibb, Ossie Clark and Zandra Rhodes, and everyone bought their clothes at Biba.'

In November 1973, who should come to play the Rainbow Room but the New York Dolls, whose Mercury debut has just been released in Britain. 'We have come to England to redeem the social outcasts,' declares David Johansen at the band's chaotic press conference. 'Everyone here seems to be . . . homosexual. Kids are finding out there isn't much difference between them sexually. They're finding out that the sexual terms – homo, bi, hetero – are just words in front of "sexual". They accuse me of transsexuality because I kissed Jerry, but I love Jerry. I think boys should kiss boys, don't you?'

'I remember the Biba's gigs, because Arthur got arrested for shoplifting,' Johansen says twenty-five years later. 'See, that scene at Biba's was very much like the Mercer Arts Center. All these people got dressed up and came out and made a thing of it. It was like, We've got this costume, where are we gonna go in it?'

London is primed for the band: the two Dolls shows, on 26 and 27 November, are *the* hot ticket on the social scene. 'We *loved* the New York Dolls, we thought they were absolutely superb,' says Nicky Chinn. 'They were everything we were doing, but much darker. We loved what was going on in America. The Americans *were* a little more extreme – they would take things that extra mile, and we were watching that a lot.' In *Melody Maker*, Michael Watts writes that the Dolls are 'a great kick in the ass to the corpus of rock 'n' roll . . . with their crude musicality and exaggerated posturing, [they] are the new children of pop, mimicking their elders and blowing rude noises'.

86

No less important than the Biba dates is the Dolls' appearance on BBC 2's *Old Grey Whistle Test*, when they perform 'Jet Boy' and 'Looking for a Kiss' as Bob Harris winces off-camera. 'I was thirteen, and it was my first real emotional experience,' Morrissey will write in the slim study of the Dolls he published in 1981; 'the next day I was twenty-one.' Being a Dolls devotee, said Morrissey, ruined his education: 'I was thrown off the track and football teams at school for turning up to games in desperately self-designed Dolls T-shirts. The teachers were very worried, and expected me to turn up for maths in drag. The Dolls gave me a sense of uniqueness, as if they were my own personal discovery. Back in '73 the Dolls were total outcasts, and no one with any sense even mentioned their name. As it was, I became the only visible proof that some actually listened to them.'

One of the many bands with whom the Dolls played in New York in the latter half of 1973 was a new group called Kiss. Like Elton John – like Cher and Bette Midler, come to that[3] – Kiss would take glam's outrageousness and repackage it very efficiently as theatre, in their case a post-Alice Cooper theatre of heavy-metal horror rock.

'Kiss actually told me they were inspired by the Dolls,' says Bob Gruen. 'They had seen the kind of girls the Dolls attracted, and Gene Simmons certainly wanted to attract girls. Gene and Ace [Frehley] both told me they went to see the Dolls at the Diplomat Hotel, and the next night they had a band discussion about their image. They figured there was no point in trying to be beautiful, because they couldn't compete with the Dolls, so they decided to be monsters – they went the other way.[4] Ace actually wore his make-up for the first time when he came to the Dolls' Hallowe'en Bash at the Waldorf-Astoria.'

As Kiss began their inexorable rise in 1974, so the New York Dolls began to fall apart. 'Bands like Kiss were professional, and that was the

3 Midler, who made her name as the high priestess of glam at a gay Manhattan establishment called the Continental Baths, was often to be seen watching the Dolls at the Mercer. Prior to his joining the band, Jerry Nolan and she had been lovers.
4 When Dave Marsh reported on the New York glam scene for *Melody Maker* in October 1973 – the month that would end up with the Waldorf Hallowe'en Bash –

difference between them and us,' says David Johansen. 'I mean, even Alice Cooper was pretty raunchy till he got rid of the band. When people have their eye on the prize – like, *We're gonna make it big!* – that's different. But we wouldn't have conversations, we would just fight: *Oh yeah? Fuck you!* The business was so different then. There were no venues, no rules, you'd make it up as you went along. And like everything else, it was co-opted.'

In a 1974 piece entitled 'Rock Goes Hol-ly-wooood!', Albert Goldman wrote that rock had become 'pure entertainment', with its major stars harking back to the campy glamour of Busby Berkeley or the Gothic ghoulishness of Bela Lugosi. By rights rock should have died, Goldman argued, but instead it had become 'an industry, a dream factory, like the Hollywood of old', serving up sounds and images of excess for the vicarious titillation of twenty-somethings who'd outgrown the ideals of the sixties. When Alice Cooper's head was guillotined on stage, what did these 'nice boys and girls in their blown-dry hair, finely fitting bell-bottoms, and cunningly applied eyeshadow' do? Why, 'break into spontaneous applause and heartily cheer', of course.

Even black stars like Patti Labelle and the Pointer Sisters were taking the traditional glamour of R&B performers to new extremes of futuristic gaudiness: the Pointers drew on the same retro mannerisms as Bette Midler, but the space-age outfits of Labelle and Nona Hendryx provided a wild contrast to the earthy lust of 'Lady Marmalade'. Nothing, however, could touch Elton John, with his white cowboy jumpsuit, marabou feathers and silver lamé hotpants – not to mention the five baby grand pianos on stage, each painted a different colour. Liberace should have been so shameless.[5]

Excess was now the name of the game. Even Lou Reed bounced back from the murk of *Berlin* with an outrageous new persona: the speed-ravaged Rock 'n' Roll Animal, a shaven-headed leather queen pumping

he wrote that Kiss looked 'as if they just stepped out of the underground movie *Pink Flamingos*, leading me to believe I was right all along in thinking that the glitter craze was an ugliness contest'.

5 Glam excess reached a pinnacle of sorts with the giant platforms John wore as the Pinball Wizard in the film version of *Tommy* (1975). As Phil Dellio and Scott Woods put it, 'Perhaps the defining image of Elton's *uber*-man status during the mid-

out cranked-up versions of his great Velvets and *Transformer* songs. 'Recording songs you'd written four years earlier and have them get popular now was pretty interesting,' he says. '*Rock 'n' Roll Animal* is still one of the best live recordings ever done. I've got enough distance on it now that I can hear it too. Those songs were *made* for that sound.' By the release of the lame *Sally Can't Dance*, Lou had become a kind of Igor, an anti-icon of Gothic heavy metal with Maltese crosses shaved into his hair (and a transsexual lover named Rachel). 'It's fabulous being a blond,' he said, 'especially when the dark roots begin to show. It's so trashy.'

But the most extreme star of American glam wasn't Lou Reed or the New York Dolls but the amazing creature who went by the name of Jobriath – the first and only performer of the era to proclaim himself 'a true fairy'. Born Bruce Campbell in 1946 in the fabulously named town of King of Prussia, Pennsylvania, Jobriath was a classically trained pianist who'd wound up playing the gay teenager Woof (yes, Woof) in the Hollywood production of *Hair*. A breakdown later, he was discovered by the impresario Jerry Brandt, who overheard a demo tape in the office of Columbia overlord Clive Davis. Davis wasn't impressed, but Brandt was convinced he'd found the American David Bowie in embryo, and that he could make him the biggest star of the decade.

'He was frail, pale, unwashed, unkempt and he smelled,' Brandt told *Rolling Stone* of the epicene boy he found living on beer in an unfurnished Hollywood apartment in late 1972. 'And he was one of the most beautiful creatures I had ever laid eyes on.' For Jobriath's signature, Brandt, who had managed Carly Simon and run the Electric Circus club in New York, succeeded in prising the unimaginable advance sum of $300,000 out of Elektra's Jac Holzman. Some of this was used to finance the recording sessions for the singer's first album at Electric Lady in New York: a collection of songs, produced by former Hendrix engineer Eddie Kramer, that drew heavily on Elton John, Bowie's *Hunky Dory* and Bob Ezrin's pseudo-classical arrangements for Alice

seventies – maybe even the defining image of the entire decade – can be found in Ken Russell's *Tommy* . . . a one-man Mount Rushmore of hyperbolic meaninglessness, a glittering *tabula rasa* for wayward pop dreamers . . .'

Cooper. Even more of the money was spent on hyping Jobriath as no one had ever been hyped before, not least on erecting a forty-one by forty-three-foot Times Square billboard that reproduced the nude photo of the singer on the cover of *Jobriath*. Shy and retiring the queen from King of Prussia wasn't.

'Jobriath is a combination of Dietrich, Marceau, Nureyev, Tchaikovsky, Wagner, Nijinksy, Bernhardt, an astronaut, the best of Jagger, Bowie, Dylan, with the glamour of Garbo,' Jerry Brandt proclaimed to the world. 'He is a singer, dancer, woman, man.' The truth was that this science-fiction satyr really was talented – a Bowie derivative, certainly, but hardly a charlatan. ('Morning Starship' alone is proof of that.) The problem was that Brandt's hype backfired horribly. Even with the *New York Times* declaring *Jobriath* to be 'a brazen parody that celebrates outrageousness for the sake of outrageousness', and *Record World* hailing the singer as 'a true Renaissance man', the PR overkill made many onlookers dismiss Jobriath as a shock-value novelty. Nor was America nearly ready to embrace a kinky rock 'n' roll faun so unambiguous about his homosexuality, as trumpeted on the album's opening 'I'maman'. When Jobriath and his band the Creatures were booked on *Midnight Special* in January 1974 – following up the infamous performances of Todd Rundgren and the New York Dolls – the show's producer demanded that they substitute 'Rock of Ages' for the *faux*-soul S&M anthem 'Take Me, I'm Yours'.

Hype-o-phobes were hardly encouraged by the news that Jobriath was going to make his live debut at the Paris Opera House – a concept green-lighted by Elektra's then closeted gay CEO, David Geffen. In the end, the show was shelved as costs became prohibitive; the singer's first live appearances instead took place in the rather more modest Bottom Line club in New York in July 1974. Not long afterwards, Jobriath's sophomore album *Creatures of the Street* was released, replete with proto-*Young Americans* funk and heavily orchestrated, Broadway-style paeans to movie stars. (The Broadway touches anticipated Jobriath's later incarnation as – in his own words – 'rum-soaked lounge singer' Cole Berlin.) Half-way through the singer's first national tour, Jerry Brandt himself wearied of the hype he'd set in motion – as well as of his protégé's increasing dependency on drugs – and dropped him like a hot potato. Tracks for a projected third Elektra album – including 'The Actor' and 'Oh Lord, I'm Bored' – were never to see the light of day.

Jobriath retired from rock in 1975, living a reclusive existence in Manhattan's Chelsea Hotel before reinventing himself as Cole Berlin at the end of the decade. He died in the hotel in 1983, one of the first victims of the AIDS epidemic that was starting to ravage America's gay community. As Rob Cochrane writes in a long-overdue appreciation of this egregious figure, 'It is somewhat telling that the only openly gay performer of that period of androgyny and shock is also the one now totally forgotten when the period is recalled'.[6]

In March 1974 the New York Dolls set to work on their second album with legendary sixties producer 'Shadow' Morton.

'Shadow was a producer I loved,' says David Johansen. 'And he would actually acquiesce to our demands, though he was fighting his own demons at the time. I remember him in the studio saying, "Boys, I'm falling off the wagon with a resounding boom!" We were like, *Yay!* I think he did a great job – "Stranded in the Jungle" was a radio record, which was no mean achievement. Shadow had all these Brill Building stories I wanted to hear – he'd been, like, the rebel of the Brill Building in a way. He'd talk me through all the Shangri-Las records he'd produced. And Janis Ian's "Society's Child": what a genius record *that* was.'

Composed of well-trodden R&B covers and new Dolls originals like 'Babylon' and 'Puss 'n Boots', *Too Much, Too Soon* was all too fitting a title for a band whose early promise was now being undone by some familiar New York snags – above all, drugs and liquor. 'The Dolls failed because they lived their rock 'n' roll fantasy,' was the terse but fair summary of Kiss's Gene Simmons, a former schoolteacher from Brooklyn. Both Johnny Thunders and Jerry Nolan were in the early stages of heroin addiction, while Arthur Kane was a hopeless drunk embroiled in an insane affair with a tough Lower East Side groupie called Connie Gripp.

To prepare the world for *Too Much, Too Soon*, the Dolls undertook an 'Easter Parade' mini-tour of Manhattan and New York's outer boroughs

6 One of Jobriath's great admirers is Morrissey, who featured him on the cover of the Japanese release of 'My Love Life'.

that culminated in a gig at Club 82, an ancient downtown joint catering to drag queens and their admirers. In deference to the club's lesbian owners Tommy and Butchie, the band played the entire set in dresses. 'We were always saying they should have rock 'n' roll in there, because the drag queen thing was out in the street now and people didn't need to hide any more,' remembers Johansen, who wore a very fetching item belonging to his girlfriend. 'Tommy said she'd give us a shot. I don't think John wore a dress, that was where he drew the line, but I was dressed like some old hooker. Girls were crying – "They really *are* gay!" – and Butchie was yelling at me from behind the bar, "I always said you was a faggot!"'[7]

Outside the city, things weren't going so well for the Dolls. One of the bands they toured with was Mott the Hoople, who had followed up *All the Young Dudes* with *Mott*, their first album to go Top Forty in America. (Mott had also replaced the departed Mick Ralphs with former Spooky Tooth guitarist Luther Grosvenor, who in the process acquired one of the great glam monickers, Ariel Bender.) 'Mott used us on that tour,' Johansen told Nick Kent. 'Ian Hunter would bring out Ariel into the audience when we were on stage and tell him to study how Johnny was moving. And after gigs we'd go up to their rooms, steal their drink, fuck their groupies and leave 'em wondering what happened.'

One could argue that Mott's greater success in America – *Too Much, Too Soon* never charted any higher than No. 167 – was testament in part to their more conservative appearance. Certainly the rise of a band like Aerosmith, who like the Dolls were represented by Leber-Krebs management, suggested that toning down the transvestism might have given the Dolls a greater chance in America. Ironically, Aerosmith's Steven Tyler was if anything more influenced by David Johansen than he was by Mick Jagger. 'I was in awe of the Dolls,' he has said. 'They used to say I was a Jagger lookalike, but Johansen had lips for miles. That guy could swallow the earth . . .

7 Many of the original Mercer Arts Center bands played Club 82 after the Mercer itself collapsed in August 1973. Among the newer acts on the scene were the Fast, the Brats, Jet Black, Another Pretty Face, the early Television and the Stilettos, featuring Debbie Harry. Here was the germ of the CBGBs punk scene.

and has!' (The following year, with *Toys in the Attic* chalking up platinum sales in America, an irate Steven Morrissey fired off a missive to *Melody Maker* decrying Aerosmith's unoriginality. 'Thanks but no thanks,' he huffed. 'I'll stick with the New York Dolls for my rock 'n' thrills.')

By the end of 1974 the combination of low morale and narcotic stupefaction was sounding the death knell for a band who'd been twenty times more innovative than Aerosmith would ever be. 'The Stones had minders and nurses, but we were on our own,' says Johansen. 'If we were in Detroit and someone needed a fix, you had to go out and deal with it.' To their rescue, supposedly, came the Dickensian figure of Malcolm McLaren, whose London shop Too Fast to Live, Too Young to Die the Dolls had patronized during their trip to England in 1973. McLaren's brainwave was to give the band a comprehensive image overhaul, dressing them in red leather and draping a hammer-and-sickle banner behind them on stage.

'Malcolm was never our manager,' says Johansen. 'He was like our haberdasher for a while, and he became enamoured of us. Me and Syl had written this song, "Red Patent Leather", so we told Malcolm we wanted red patent-leather outfits, and he came over from England with them. He kind of travelled around with us, because he was on the outs with Vivienne [Westwood] and she wanted him to have some space. But I liked him, I liked his politics. He was somebody I could talk to because he had a frame of reference, he knew about the French Revolution. Try to talk to John about that, forget about it. But it was really over by then; Malcolm was only there for the last month or six weeks.'

Unveiled at New York's Little Hippodrome on 28 February 1975, the 'Red Patent Leather' show was greeted with a mixture of disbelief and relief that the Dolls were at least in sync with each other. The plastic Marxism was crass, but new songs like 'On Fire' and 'Teenage News' were at least coherent. Unfortunately, this wasn't enough to keep the band from imploding. 'I was disappointed with the fact that much of their behaviour was wasted energy,' said McLaren. 'It was just a trashy energy, easily disposable . . . an energy that didn't really bear any point of view except jealousy, which is so time wasting.' It didn't help that both Thunders and Nolan thought McLaren was a twit.[8]

The end came with a mini-tour booked in late April in the Dolls' old stomping ground of southern Florida. Desperate to get back to their heroin supply in New York, Thunders and Nolan announced that they were quitting the band. Though Johansen and Sylvain struggled with an augmented line-up which took them to Japan that July, the Dolls were effectively dead. Their legacy, however, would live on for decades, sowing the seeds of New York punk and influencing an untold number of glammed-up hard rockers in the eighties. 'What the Dolls did was show a lot of people, "Hey, I can make a band,"' says Johansen. 'It showed that you don't have to woodshed in your room and come out ten years later as Eric Clapton.'

By late 1975 New York was poised on the brink of punk, with the Heartbreakers formed and a new undercurrent of bands dispensing with all traces of glam. 'I can remember we were rehearsing and the Ramones were down the hall, they hadn't played yet,' recalls Johansen. 'We told them, "Oh, God, you guys suck so bad, forget about it!" But I was like that with everybody. I'd say to Chris Frantz, "You're really a nice kid, you should get into some kind of business." I'd say, "With that guy singin', you're not gonna get anywhere." So what do I know?'

'Glitter rock was about decadence – platform shoes and boys in eye make-up, David Bowie and androgyny,' wrote Legs McNeil in *Please Kill Me!*. '[It was about] rich rock stars living their lives from Christopher Isherwood's Berlin stories. You know, Sally Bowles hanging out with drag queens, drinking champagne for breakfast and having *ménages à trois* while the Nazis slowly grab the power.' Compared to what was happening in the real world, McNeil argued, 'decadence seemed kind of quaint'. Punk wasn't about decay, it was about apocalypse *now*.

In some senses, this is too simplistic. While Dick Hebdige was right in his *Subculture* to argue that 'the punk aesthetic . . . can be read

8 Even as the Dolls were going through their death throes, McLaren was catching a sneak preview of the future: the support act at the Little Hippodrome was Television, whose Richard Hell wore a ripped T-shirt and safety pins. By May 1975, Hell would be playing bass in Johnny Thunders's new band, the Heartbreakers.

as an attempt to expose glam rock's implicit contradictions', and that 'the "working classness" . . . of punk ran directly counter to the arrogance, elegance & verbosity of the glam-rock superstars', even he conceded that the dog collars and bondage tartan trousers were really just another set of costumes – a kind of inverted dandyism through self-defilement. 'Punk thus represents a deliberately scrawled addendum to the "text" of glam rock,' Hebdidge concluded, 'one designed to puncture glam rock's extravagantly ornate style.' Punk, in a nutshell, was glam ripping itself apart.

Even the Ramones descended directly from glam. 'I was into dressing up in my own style,' says Joey Ramone (a.k.a. Jeffrey Hyman), who sang in a Queens glam band called Sniper. 'I had a black satin jumpsuit made of stretch material with a bullet chain hanging around the groin with the zipper open, and elbow-length black leather gloves and a chain. I had pink-lavender boots with six-inch platform heels, a leather jacket, black sunglasses, long hair. It was pretty androgynous, but in those days you could let go. Still, a lot of people wanted to kill me.'

'Joey really got into the glitter thing,' recalled his brother, Mickey. 'He was stealing all my mother's jewellery, her clothes, her make-up and her scarves. I thought it was great that Joey was in a band, but it was really dangerous to hitchhike down Queens Boulevard looking the way he did. In platform boots he was over seven feet tall.' Joey did eventually get beaten up, but not before Sniper had become mainstays of the main local club, the Coventry. 'It was a real glitter crowd,' said Mickey Hyman. 'Everyone was into the Harlots of 42nd Street.' Both the Dolls and Kiss were regular attractions at the Coventry.

In the summer of 1974, with glam on the wane, Joey formed the Slade–Stooges hybrid that became the Ramones. Within weeks, the band had distilled the essence of seventies hard rock down to two-minute blasts of proto-punk bubblegum – Brill Building meets nihilist metal. After the Velvets and the Dolls, they were the next stage in the continuum that defined New York's punk sensibility. And when Joey put his mom's make-up back in her boudoir and invested in some ripped Levi's and sneakers, the city's romance with glam was over.

'Just as Nirvana would come along and blow away the hair bands, so the Ramones came along and blew away the glam bands,' says Bebe Buell. 'And then Malcolm McLaren took our Dolls and Ramones and turned them into the Sex Pistols.'

tumbling down

'sunset, end of my dreams . . .'
Roxy Music

Freddie Mercury and girlfriend Mary Austin, backstage at the Rainbow Theatre, 1974

In Britain glitter pop was still going strong through the first half of 1974: the Sweet hit with 'Teenage Rampage', Suzi Quatro with 'Devil Gate Drive' and Gary Glitter with 'Remember Me This Way'. There were new pretenders rising through the Bell and RAK ranks, too: the Arrows with 'A Touch Too Much' (and its B-side, 'I Love Rock 'n' Roll', later a giant hit for Joan Jett), the Rubettes with the drippy 'Sugar Baby Love', the Bay City Rollers with 'Remember (Sha-La-La)' and 'Shang-a-Lang'.

But David Bowie, one of glam's chief architects, was fast outgrowing the genre, creating in *Diamond Dogs* what Charles Shaar Murray described as 'the final nightmare of the glitter apocalypse'. Produced by Tony Visconti and released in April 1974, the album was *Ziggy Stardust* crossed with Burroughs's *Wild Boys*, an overwrought Orwellian song cycle set in a dystopian Manhattan of the future and written in a state of coked-out paranoia. 'Most of the songs are obscure tangles of perversion, degradation, fear and self-pity,' wrote Eric Emerson of the Magic Tramps in a *Rolling Stone* review. 'Are they masturbatory fantasies, guilt-ridden projections, terrified premonitions, or is it all Alice Cooper exploitation?' A quarter-century later, it's still hard to answer that question.

In June, Bowie took *Diamond Dogs* on the road, using the biggest stage show ever mounted in rock history – a six-ton, $250,000 set depicting the 'Hunger City' in which the album is set. Even Tony DeFries worried that things had gone too far this time, though he himself was hardly helping matters with the chronic overspending at MainMan's New York office. Half-way through the US tour, moreover, Bowie decided to scrap the whole set and start again, re-emerging in September as an anorexic matinée idol in tight-cut jacket and baggy trousers – the world's first glimpse of the 'plastic soul' man who would be heard to full effect on 1975's *Young Americans*.

For Bowie, the tour seems to have spelled the end of glam as we fans knew it. When the shoddy, hurriedly recorded *David Live* was released in October 1974, it horrified him. '*David Live* was the final death of Ziggy,' he later reflected. 'The tension it contains must be like a vampire's teeth coming down on you. And that photo on the cover! My God, it looks as if I've just stepped out of the grave.'

Back in London, coincidentally, the charts were being graced by the Bowie-esque strains of a band called Cockney Rebel, fronted by the self-aggrandizing Steve Harley. On their first hits – 'Judy Teen' and 'Mr Soft' – Harley fused *Hunky Dory* Bowie with a camp Ray Davies-meets-Ian Hunter vocal style, topped off with arrangements that emulated early Roxy Music. But the group's very first single, 'Sebastian', was a glam masterpiece, with Harley's histrionic vocal bolstered by an epic orchestral arrangement. Nobody could quite decide if Cockney Rebel's *Clockwork Orange* rock was rebellious or simply camp – Janet Street-Porter yelled 'Rubbish!' when they played Biba's Rainbow Room – but there was a great sense of theatre in the albums *The Human Menagerie* and *The Psychomodo*. After Harley split from the group's first line-up in July 1974, he returned with a new Cockney Rebel and scored a No. 1 hit with 'Make Me Smile (Come Up and See Me)' in January 1975.

Other mavericks who rode in on glam's coat-tails included the Sensational Alex Harvey Band, fronted by a veteran Glaswegian who dubbed himself 'The Last of the Teenage Idols' and specialized in melodramatic versions of Jacques Brel songs ('Next') and Broadway standards ('The Impossible Dream'), and Ron and Russ Mael of Sparks, who had been child actors in Hollywood before making albums like the boldly titled *A Woofer in Tweeter's Clothing* (1972). In 1974 the Maels moved to London and recorded the fabulous *Kimono My House*, whose stupendous first single, 'This Town Ain't Big Enough for Both of Us', sounded like Roxy Music with hysterically camp falsetto vocals. As an eccentric double act – long-haired pretty-boy Russ contrasting with the stone-faced, Chaplinesque Ron – the brothers anticipated everyone from Soft Cell to the Pet Shop Boys.

Of course, no act got away with camp in quite the way Queen did. Looking back, Freddie Mercury was glam's purloined letter: his queerness, like the name of his band, was so in-your-face that no one even noticed it. 'They were so obviously the extremity of camp, these four little fellas looking as queer as clockwork oranges,' says Mick Rock, who took the famous picture that adorns the cover of *Queen II*. 'And yet they weren't. Even Freddie at that point lived with a girlfriend, and his main stance was heterosexual.'

Heterosexual the stance may have been, but Mercury – born Farokh Bulsara in, of all places, Zanzibar – was far from straight; even his girlfriend, Biba floor manageress Mary Austin, knew that. Indeed, Austin had much to do with Freddie's aggressively androgynous look, encouraging him to tease his hair and wear black nail polish. Not that he wasn't already a certified London dandy, having adopted the foppish fashions of his idol Jimi Hendrix as early as 1967. (Drawings he made of Hendrix in the late sixties depict the guitarist as an eighteenth-century beau with a cane.) When Mercury and Roger Taylor took over a stall in Kensington Market – a stone's throw from Biba – his effeminate style became even more extreme. 'Roger and I go poncing about and ultrablagging just about everywhere,' he wrote to a friend in 1969. 'Lately we're being termed as a couple of queens.' ('Glam was really an all-encompassing thing that segued out of the hippie thing and festered in Kensington Market,' points out Mick Rock. 'It started with all those old, glammy clothes people would wear. Even Biba came out of the hippie thing.')

In April 1970, far from ignorant of the word's connotations, Mercury and Taylor formed Queen with guitarist Brian May. ('It's ever so regal,' said Freddie of the name.) When the line-up was completed by bass player John Deacon, the group set about turning themselves into an ersatz Led Zeppelin – a blues-based hard-rock band with the fruitiest frontman in show business. But it wasn't long before Freddie Mercury was picking up tips from fellow androgynes like David Bowie and wearing outrageous one-piece body suits. Though a record deal finally came Queen's way in 1973, they didn't make the charts until the following year, when 'Seven Seas of Rhye' scraped the Top Ten and the glorious 'Killer Queen' reached No. 2. 'It's about a high-class call girl,' Mercury said of 'Killer Queen'. 'I'm trying to say that classy people can be whores too.' Insiders knew the killer queen was also a transsexual self-portrait of the regal Freddie Mercury.

'She keeps Moët et Chandon/In her pretty cabinet/ 'Let them eat cake,' she says/Just like Marie Antoinette . . .'

It was Mercury's influence which steered the band away from their Zeppelin leanings for long enough to craft this classic pop single. 'People are used to hard-rock, energy music from Queen,' he said, 'yet

A gallery of glitter rogues: *clockwise from top,* Dave Hill and Noddy Holder (Slade), Brian Connolly and Steve Priest (Sweet) and El Gaz himself

The New York Dolls, Mercer Arts Center, 1972

Below: Jobriath   *Opposite:* Alice Cooper

Steve Harley:
Biba's, London, 1974

The mighty Kiss: Gene Simmons, Ace Frehley, Peter Criss, Paul Stanley

Who's a pretty group, then? Queen and boa, *clockwise from top*: John Deacon,
Brian May, Freddie Mercury, Roger Taylor

Top: David Bowie, from the *Pin-Ups* sessions

Beyond Liberace: Elton John

Rodney's English Disco,
Hollywood Boulevard

Rodney with Eno (*right*)
at the club

English Disco vixens

Rocky Horror Picture Show:
Frank'n'Furter and Riff Raff

Ewan McGregor as Curt Wild
in *Velvet Goldmine,* 1998

this single, you almost expect Noël Coward to sing it. It's one of those bowler-hat, black-suspender-belt numbers.'

'They were almost glam rock,' said Queen publicist Tony Brainsby. 'They had elements of it, but it was on a higher, much more sophisticated level.' Which is only another way of saying that Queen had their sights set on more than periodic *Top of the Pops* appearances. In the studio they were ambitious to the point of grandiosity, working in stacked ELO-style vocals and rococo classical flourishes. On the road, Queen supported Mott the Hoople as the New York Dolls had done, but fared a lot better; by March 1975, 'Killer Queen' was in the American Top Twenty.

And then, in the summer of that year – the year when Biba closed down – Queen made the record that became glam's epic swansong. Nearly six minutes long, and accompanied by a video which aired on *Top of the Pops* for ever and ever, 'Bohemian Rhapsody' was the most over-the-top rock operetta since 'Stairway to Heaven', a multi-tracked *grand bouffe* of Wagnerian proportions. Here were all of glam's swishy mannerisms, compressed histrionics and swooning excesses, raised to fever pitch. By January 1976 it had sold over a million copies.

Of course, glam ended long before 'Bohemian Rhapsody'. '(Whatever Happened to the) Teenage Dream?' Marc Bolan asked plaintively in February 1974, when Alice Cooper's similarly themed 'Teenage Lament '74' was still in the charts. 'Did you see the suits and the platform boots?' asked Ian Hunter in the elegaic 'Saturday Gigs', the first Mott the Hoople single to feature new guitarist Mick Ronson – and unfortunately the last the group ever released.[1] Even Bowie's 'Rebel Rebel' was taken in some quarters as a lament for glam's golden days.

At Rodney Bingenheimer's English Disco, where 'Rebel Rebel' was virtually the national anthem, the writing was on the wall by the autumn of 1974. 'The really great scenes die,' reflected Tom Ayres in 1992. 'Besides, the glam culture never really took hold in the US. Slade

---

1 Among the many MainMan projects of 1974 was the solo debut by Mick Ronson, *Slaughter on Tenth Avenue*, featuring the sublime 'Hey Ma, Get Papa' – one of the very few songs credited to Bowie/Ronson.

never had a hit; Suzi Quatro and Gary Glitter had one apiece. And David Bowie? He put on a suit and went funk.' By this time, said Silverhead's Michael Des Barres, 'the sequins were lying in the gutter . . . it was October '74 and it had all come and gone so fast that everybody was burned out'.

There was one final glam bash held in Los Angeles – the 'Hollywood Street Revival and Dance', staged at the Palladium on 11 October. Paying homage to the prescient 'Death of Hippie' march in San Francisco seven years before, this 'Death of Glitter' night – so dubbed by Kim Fowley – was a valiant attempt to kill glam before the media had finished it off. Starring Iggy Pop, the New York Dolls and Silverhead, it was nothing short of a wake for the whole English Disco scene. 'All over Hollywood that night it was glitter,' recalled Chuckie Star, a fixture of Rodney's. 'The line to get into the Palladium was incredible. Everyone in LA knew it was their last chance to wear platform shoes and eyeshadow. This was *it*! Surfers from Malibu were there in midriff shirts, silver space boots, and blue eye make-up, hugging their girlfriends as they waited to get in.'

When the Dolls had finished the show with 'Personality Crisis', Star was carried on stage in a lidless glitter coffin. As the coffin passed through the revellers, Star's chest was strewn with glitter and roses. 'By definition it was all kind of tragic,' Michael Des Barres reminisced. 'But so what? There wasn't the pressure we have today; rock 'n' roll had yet to become corporate. Anything provocative was possible back then. What was so great about the glam era was that it was showbiz, but it was *tainted* showbiz.'

In time the Rodney's crowd would give birth to LA's very own protopunk scene, with Bingenheimer himself playing a key role as a DJ on KROQ. Kim Fowley would package the Quatro-esque Runaways, Jane Wiedlin would form the Go-Gos and Joan Jett would record the Arrows' 'I Love Rock 'n' Roll'. It was the fans' turn to be stars.

As the dying strains of glam were being heard in Hollywood, so the glitter scene was screeching to a halt in London. By the end of 1974 all the great glitter acts – Gary Glitter, Slade, Suzi Quatro – had made their last memorable records.

'Subconsciously, it was as if we anticipated the end of glam,' says Nicky Chinn. 'It's interesting to note that in July 1975, as glam was ending, we had a No. 3 hit with Smokie's "If You Think You Know How to Love Me", which was everything *but* glam rock – it was a ballad. I think the transition for us, musically, was quite easy, and a positive one. But as a lifestyle transition, I think we missed it quite a lot. In the end, Sweet left us because they wanted to do their own thing. *Desolation Boulevard* was really our stab at getting them taken more seriously. "The Six Teens" wasn't a glam-rock record, in many ways. And that was absolutely fine; I was certainly much happier with the reasons why Sweet left us than the reasons why Mud left us. Mud left for money and I think they paid the price. So maybe glam ended for us before it actually ended, because all our bands were leaving. I mean, it was no coincidence that Mike Chapman moved to America in 1975.'

'Glam sort of faded out, didn't it?' says Brian Eno. 'I can't remember a moment at which I thought, That's not really happening any more, but I can remember getting my hair cut, and it was quite a big moment. It must have been at the end of 1974, because I'd had it cut by the time *Another Green World* came out. Long hair for me had been a big sign of something: it had all those connotations of rebellion. Of course by 1974 it didn't have those connotations at all.'[2]

In a sense, the problem was this: that just as glam had been co-opted by Kiss and Bette Midler in America, so in Britain it had become such a part of the cultural bloodstream that it had ceased to shock. With Richard O'Brien's *Rocky Horror Show* packing them into the Royal Court's upstairs theatre, the absorption of glam's androgyny was complete. Lou Reed singing 'Walk on the Wild Side' was one thing, but Tim Curry's Frank 'n' Furter pouting 'Sweet Transvestite' – 'every homophobe's dream/nightmare', as Wayne Studer wrote in *Rock on the Wild Side* – was a travesty. Like Kiss and – a little later – the Tubes, *The Rocky Horror Show* simply diluted the original outrage of the Ridiculous Theater companies, as well as the films of Warhol and John Waters. As

2 In Eric Tamm's *Brian Eno: His Music and the Vertical Color of Sound* (1989), Eno says that 'critics' couldn't stand his ambient records: 'In their search for eternal adolescence they still want it all to be spunky and manic, [whereas] I'm interested in the idea of feeling like a very young child . . . I'm not interested in feeling like a teenager.'

Phil Dellio and Scott Woods put it in their entertaining *I Wanna be Sedated: Pop Music in the Seventies*, 'The Tubes and *The Rocky Horror Show* dealt the genre a serious blow by trying to satirize something that was partly conceived as satire from the outset.'[3] Much less tacky was Andrew Logan's annual Alternative Miss World, in which men and women, competing on equal terms, took cross-dressing to new extremes of perverse exoticism.

Glitter dribbled on into 1975, with hits by the Sweet ('Fox on the Run'), Gary Glitter ('Doin' All Right with the Boys'), Kenny ('Fancy Pants') and the Rubettes ('I Can Do It'). But the giant teen sensation of the day was the Bay City Rollers, who had notched up four Top Ten hits the previous year and now scored two No. 1s ('Bye Bye Baby' and 'Give a Little Love') on the trot. Originally signed to Bell in 1971, when they had a one-off hit with their Jonathan King-produced cover of the Gentrys' 'Keep On Dancing', the Rollers were a quintet of sexless Scotsmen in tartan baggies and platforms packaged by an astute gay manager named Tam Paton. *New Musical Express* called them 'assembly-line androids in clown outfits', but the little girls screamed and fainted all over again. Paton's genius lay in understanding that the androgyny of glam rock had run its course – that what fourteen-year-old girls wanted now was (in the words of confessed Rollermaniac Sheryl Garratt) 'slim, unthreatening, baby-faced types who looked more like themselves'. Rollermania even caught on briefly in America, when 'Saturday Night' became a No. 1 hit in November 1975.

From T. Rex's 'Ride a White Swan' to the Rollers' 'Bye Bye Baby': had pop really become so unadventurous in the space of five years? Well, yes. But it didn't help that Marc Bolan himself had become such a comical self-parody, churning out feeble singles like 'Light of Love' (1974) and unspeakable albums like *Bolan's Zip-Gun* (1975) – the musical evidence of his dissipation in the far-flung cities of Los Angeles and Monte Carlo. 'He took time to go to Monte Carlo and that was like la-la-land, so he lost touch,' B. P. Fallon told Pamela Des Barres.

3 Ironically, the 1975 movie version of the show, which failed in Britain, was a cult hit in America, giving birth to the audience participation craze that accompanied its screening for many years afterwards. Thus, in bastardized form, did glam live on.

'Hanging out with Ringo, gambling every night, isn't going to tell you much about the music scene, is it?'

Coked to the gills and terrified of the way fame (in Mark Volman's words) was 'skirting away from him', Bolan became increasingly defensive. 'I haven't slipped, not in my chart,' he said. 'I'm still number one. If you go back nine months, I said then, "Glam rock is dead." Now a lot of bands are having problems with their image, adjusting to the changes in the world. Fortunately for me, I'm not involved in that any more because I made my statement clear at the time. I started the first teen wave, but I didn't want to get cemented in that environment.'

In the last years of his life, Bolan was saved by television – first in the form of Mike Mansfield's pop show *Supersonic*, and then through his very own kiddie-pop show, *Marc*. With his best album since *The Slider*, 1977's *Dandy in the Underworld*, the 'porky pixie' bestirred himself to seize the pop moment one more time. (A tour with the Damned had Marc proclaiming himself 'the elder statesman of punk, the godfather of punk', and *Marc* would serve as a showcase for several up-and-coming bands, including Generation X and the Boomtown Rats.)

Watching Bolan on *Marc* was mesmerizing: on the one hand, it seemed horribly undignified, but on the other, it defined what was great about the man in the first place – his ability simply to revel in the evanescent charisma of stardom. 'Bolan's pop music was impermanent,' reflected Paul Morley in 1980. 'He made it so because he recognized that the pop song was a moment, a mark in time, at most a period. He knew that the pop star, through the very nature of the phenomenon, faded away.' Watching *Marc*, said Morley, 'it's as if he's masochistically rubbing in the fact that as a pop person he was essentially *passé*, half-heartedly indulging in being a pop personality'.

What, one wonders, could have been more masochistic than inviting David Bowie to be a guest on the final *Marc* show? Here was the former Ziggy Stardust, the former Thin White Duke, the man who'd brilliantly reinvented himself as a Berliner fallen to earth, sharing the mike with the underworld dandy who'd been left behind and washed up on the shores of children's TV. Duetting on a hastily written song called 'Standing Next to You', the two men had barely started when Bolan tripped over a wire and toppled off the stage. Could there have been a more painfully symbolic end to the Electric Warrior's career?

Bolan died just a week later when a purple mini driven by his common-law wife Gloria Jones swerved into a tree in Barnes, near the couple's Richmond home. 'I'd hate to go now,' he had told Steve Harley just a month earlier. 'I'd only get a paragraph on page three.' He is still one of the great pop stars.

out: crush with eyeliner

'All this time later, it still raises its brightly coloured head . . .'
David Bowie, 1987

Futurist Amazon: Patti Labelle

Glam rock may have petered out – or simply been superseded, by blue-collar messiahs like Bruce Springsteen as much as by the bilious nihilists of punk – but its lipstick traces were everywhere you looked.[1] Not least in the world of black music.

Glamour and dandyism had always been central to black culture, but no one had seen black fashions like those sported in the blaxploiting seventies. 'All the young aces and dudes are out there lolly-gagging around in front of the Monterey club,' observed Tom Wolfe in his 1974 essay 'Funky But Chic'. They were 'wearing their two-tone patent Pyramids with the five-inch heels that swell out at the bottom to match the Pierre Chareau Art Deco plaid bell-bottom baggies they have on . . . all of them, every ace, every dude, out there just *getting over* in the baddest possible way . . . so that somehow the sons of the slums have become the Brummells and Gentlemen of Leisure, the true fashion plates of the 1970s . . .'

The continuum from Little Richard to Sly Stone to the super-pimp style of Wolfe's ghetto fops was wild enough, but the *outré* outfits of soul acts like Labelle and funk collectives like Parliament-Funkadelic looked as if they'd come from another galaxy. Particularly outrageous was Labelle's Nona Hendryx, whose favourite garment was a white cat-suit with a sequinned triangle at the crotch and a pair of silver hand-cuffs dangling from a belt. For Patti Labelle herself, the choice seemed to be a straight one between girl-group nostalgia – revival shows – and a kind of Amazonian futurism. 'The costumes are just a come-on, like a glittery sign,' she told Charles Shaar Murray. 'Then people read the sign and see what's on it.'

Space-age glam also played a large part in the look of P-Funk. George Clinton was funk's own Roy Wood, while Bootsy Collins – the rhinestone-encrusted overlord of space bass – was the Sweet's Steve Priest on Pimpmobile overdrive. Coming out of acid-fried, Sly-inspired hippiedom, P-Funk took soul's sartorial excesses further than any other black group, donning wings, capes and knee-length platforms (not to

1 Note that certain bands of the punk era – for example, the Only Ones – continued to mine the seam of decadent androgyny first struck by Lou Reed and others. The mascara-smeared Peter Perrett was a direct descendant of these Baudelairean trouba-dours.

mention diapers) when Motown acts were still experimenting with loon pants. The P-Funk image helped to turn a bunch of ghetto clowns into avatars of a black avant-garde, and every funk act from Rick James to Earth, Wind and Fire followed in their tracks.

The most innovative black star of the eighties, Prince, drew explicitly on glam rock, going so far as to write a song called 'Glam Slam', and then naming a club after it. Whether or not it was conscious, the pointed kinkiness and bisexuality of *Dirty Mind* came directly from glam, as did the loudly trumpeted 'Controversy', with its central question: 'Am I black or white? Am I straight or gay?' For all its studied *Rocky Horror Show* transvestism, Prince's narcissistic androgyny was certainly the most hypnotic thing *this* writer had seen since Marc Bolan. Like Presley and Jagger, Prince was half-man, half-woman, a kind of god-like hermaphrodite. When, a decade later, he changed his 'name' to a hybrid sign combining the male and female symbols, it seemed a logical conclusion to the question of not only his own sexual identity but that of Bolan, Bowie and all the other heroes of glam rock.[2]

In the mid- to late seventies, with rock polarized between airbrushed album-oriented rock and monochrome punk, glamour went back underground, to the lurid chic of disco. Here, gays and street freaks could reclaim the rituals of exhibitionism and élitism, which was why the newly moneyed Warhol crowd were so quick to adopt Manhattan's Studio 54 as their shrine. 'We want it to be bisexual – very, very bisexual,' announced 54-owner Steve Rubell, and it was. Here again were mirrors and silver clothes and coke-crazed narcissists, together with a bevy of androgynous new stars like Grace Jones. 'Once again, pop music is unabashedly gay,' Albert Goldman could write once disco had been blown wide open with *Saturday Night Fever*. 'With the war in Vietnam abandoned, the Emperor Dick deposed and the dread recession rolled back, pop music is no longer dedicated to strident-voiced, Dylanesque tirades about the way things are.'

2 Anyone who doubts the impact of black glam on American culture need only look at basketball's 'bad boy' Dennis Rodman, the Chicago Bulls guard who wears violet eyeshadow, dyes stars into his hair and boasts of bisexual exploits. To promote his 1996 autobiography, *Bad As I Wanna Be*, Rodman turned up at a Fifth Avenue bookstore in a wedding dress.

In the early eighties, reacting against the gloom of post-punk bands like Joy Division, glam once again poked its head into the air. This time it took the form of the generation who'd grown up on Bowie and Bolan, and who were now ready to have some stylish fun again. Some of the stars were punk rejects – Adam Ant, for example – while others were former Ziggy kids who'd started 'Bowie nights' at London clubs like Billy's and Blitz. 'Such a new puritanism has grown up of late,' Adam told *The Face* in April 1981. 'I'd rather dress up like Liberace.'

'Looking around, you can see punks and art students and soul boys and transvestites and freelance oddballs all dressed, not necessarily to kill, but definitely to be noticed,' wrote Dave Rimmer about a Blitz night in early 1980. (Among the throng, Rimmer noted, were such key scene-makers of the original glam era as Andrew Logan and Duggie Fields.) Out of this incestuous in-crowd came the New Romantic stars – both great and small – who dominated the first half of the eighties. Stars like Boy George, who'd camped outside Bowie's Haddon Hall in 1973 and greeted the Thin White Duke on his arrival at Victoria Station in May 1976. Like the Blitz doorman Steve Strange, who appeared in Bowie's 'Ashes to Ashes' video. Like Marilyn, the beautiful Monroe impersonator who would manage one hit ('Calling Your Name') in the wake of Culture Club mania. All of these stars were reviving the glitzy fun of their own teenage years, when Ziggy Stardust had made them feel they weren't alone in the world.[3]

The first New Romantic success was Spandau Ballet, a group whose 'glamour' was so codified and self-important that it came across as hopelessly campy. More enduring was the music of Japan, an immaculate Bowie/Roxy composite, and of ABC, who revived Roxy's smart irony with the gold-lamé funk of 1982's *Lexicon of Love*. Culture Club themselves became one of the most successful pop groups in the world, racking up six Top Ten hits in America in the space of fourteen months. Boy George's secret lay in taking the androgyny of glam a stage further, turning himself into a kind of cuddly eunuch. More influential was the female androgyny of the Eurythmics' Annie Lennox, which did for

3 Bowie himself was only too pleased to play godfather to the new pop: his 'Fashion' (1980) was a New Romantic anthem.

white pop what Grace Jones had done for black disco: more audacious was the pervy 'deviance' of Soft Cell's Marc Almond. The visual element with all of these performers was heightened by the new prominence of video as a marketing tool.

'Glam is back,' wrote Jon Savage in June 1983. 'Much of it is, like a decade ago, the surface style for a new age of frivolity – making videos while Great Britain polarizes – and musical soma: what better than to accompany the synthetic allure of fizzy pop with surrealist, dream-like images of weird sex out of the ad factory. This is Blitz culture gone admass; the Blitz obsession with the "feminine", a fast-moving, sharply defined exotic surface image with a total *lack* of any commitment, has defined the terms under which most modern pop groups operate . . .'[4]

Despite the 'glamour' of Madonna – a glamour overtly inspired by gays and transsexuals – America never produced its own versions of these invading British androgynes. 'America will never develop a Boy George, just as Britain will never develop a Creedence Clearwater Revival,' says Kim Fowley. 'America needs to have John Wayne masculinity in everything it does – radio in particular.' (This, says Fowley, is why the 'tubercular' Jobriath was doomed to fail.) What America did do was to pick up where the New York Dolls had left off – or rather, where Kiss and the Tubes and *The Rocky Horror Show* had left off. (The Tubes' hyperbolic frontman Fee Waybill, with his glam *alter ego* Quay Lewd resplendent in ten-inch silver platforms, was simply a mainstream dilution of the act Wayne County had been doing in New York for years.)

'Glam rock reappeared with Poison in 1985,' says Kim Fowley. 'This wasn't the same as the glitter movement in the seventies. The only things that were the same were the lipstick, the eyeliner, the female make-up on males. So it took ten years from the end of Rodney's Disco for make-up to come back in LA. And then Poison begat a giant list of men wearing make-up from that point on. Even Guns 'N' Roses wore make-up at one point.'

4 A decade later, glam resurfaced yet again in a short-lived revival of New Romanticism itself. 'This is not retro,' claimed 'Romo' DJ Simon Price. 'It's a revolution against drab Britpop complacency, a flash-dash towards style, poise, chic, mystique, glamour.' So, *not* retro, then . . .

From the Finnish band Hanoi Rocks to Sunset Strip clowns like Quiet Riot, who reached No. 5 in America with their 1983 version of Slade's 'Cum On Feel the Noize', glam metal was a bastardized form of rock androgyny that completely bypassed genuine sexual deviance. By the end of the eighties, the 'big hair bands' had become mere parodies of something intended to be parodic in the first place. They talked loudly about 'doing their own thing', but really they were doing everything by numbers. Even the more Gothic groups – drawing on seventies icons like Alice Cooper and Ozzy Osborne – plotted their careers with the meticulousness of law students. The rest, from Poison to lesser-known entities like London, were doing little more than reworking old Van Halen riffs.

'Make-up brings out the bisexual tendencies, because women do like women, no matter what people say,' opined a metal groupie in Penelope Spheeris's hilarious film *The Decline of Western Civilization, Part Two: The Metal Years* (1988), about the 'big hair' scene in LA. Another girl in the film said that 'guys in the metal scene are fun because you can take advantage of them as they take advantage of you', while an androgynous male headbanger claimed that 'a lotta guys whistle at me'. Yet ultimately, gays on the metal scene experienced the same rock-jock homophobia, and 'heavy metal chicks' made little effort to be anything more than Frederick's of Hollywood mannequins come to life.

In the end, a twin-pronged assault by thrash metal and grunge killed off the pouting hair-trees: punk rock had finally hit America, and it was time to shed the mascara and hair lacquer. In Spheeris's film, a Megadeth fan defined a headbanger as someone 'who doesn't accept glam in any way'. By the time Nirvana's *Nevermind* was in the Top Ten in 1991, glam metal was finished. Yet even in the brave new world of alternative rock, androgyny and transvestism reappeared: Kurt Cobain and Evan Dando wore dresses, and Jane's Addiction were a walking jumble sale of cross-dressed fashions, like Boy George in a tumble dryer with the Red Hot Chilli Peppers. Even U2, striving to change their image as earnest purveyors of epic rock, glammed themselves up in kinky old Berlin and recorded the surprisingly playful *Achtung Baby* (1991). When the band went on the *Zooropa* tour,

Bono was wearing make-up and a gold-lamé jacket.[5]

Glam rock as a musical style refuses to go away, even when the bands who use it eschew the obvious use of glamour. The Smiths borrowed both riffs and homoerotic themes from glam, and Dolls devotee Morrissey frequently referenced it as quintessential pop, even hiring Mick Ronson to produce *Your Arsenal* in 1992. That year, moreover, a new band hit the headlines with almost the same impact the Smiths had had eight years before: Suede, a group who drew heavily on the sweeping drama of Bowie's *Ziggy Stardust*, and whose astounding first single, 'The Drowners', sounded as if it had been concocted from out-takes of 'Starman' and 'All the Young Dudes'. After the E'd-up lad-dishness of the Madchester scene and the primal howling of grunge, the swooning languorousness of Suede gave British pop the same jolt Bowie and Bolan had given it twenty years before.[6]

'We've been compared to all these people from the seventies, but it's more by accident than by design,' Suede's Brett Anderson told me at the time. 'I mean, I listened to my sister's Bowie records, but as a band we were probably more influenced by groups like the Pretenders, who were just a straight band making incredible pop records for radio.' Given that Suede were desperate to distance themselves from a bunch of markedly inferior 'glam' bands like Fabulous and Sweet Jesus (and, for that matter, the reviled Nancy Boy), one could understand Anderson's reluctance to be pigeonholed with them – or even with more artful entities like former Felt leader Lawrence Hayward's Denim. (Suede seemed to make a point of dressing in dark, nondescript

5 The Manic Street Preachers were another essentially macho band who flirted with glam trappings – or at least, in the sceptical view of Simon Reynolds and Joy Press, 'attempted to appropriate feminine "privileges" of narcissism and self-adornment while marginalizing women as subject matter of, and subjects within, rock 'n' roll'.
6 It wasn't too long afterwards that the histrionic Gothic glam of Placebo made its first appearance on the English pop scene. The band's 1996 debut included songs like 'Teenage Angst' and 'Nancy Boy' (about a transvestite). Other groups who have consciously used glam as a style include Mansun, Spacehog, Vaganza, 10 Speed and Plastico. If the existence of these groups wasn't enough, the renewed interest in glam stirred by Todd Haynes' film *Velvet Goldmine*, as well as by the off-Broadway play *Hedwig and the Angry Inch*, should be enough to bury the studied shabbiness of alternative rock for at least a couple of years.

clothes.) A couple of months later, Anderson argued that the word glam 'implies a certain shallowness', and that he liked to think 'we're a lot deeper and more emotional than that'.

But just as Anderson's fey, theatrical singing came from Bowie, so his epicene prettiness hailed from the same wellspring as Ziggy Stardust's. 'There's a forthright, *lungeing* side to pop music,' he told me, 'but there's also an inherent femininity. A lot of the time I do feel quite feminine, and it just seems to come through in the music.' Anderson even went so far as to make a Bowie-esque statement in the music press about being 'a bisexual man who's never had a homosexual experience'.

If Suede's second album, *Dog Man Star*, was *Diamond Dogs* filtered through Smashing Pumpkins art-rock, then the band's return after the acrimonious departure of guitarist Bernard Butler was unabashed glam. From the euphoric 'Trash' to the bleakly melancholy 'By the Sea', *Coming Up* (1996) was the logical extension of the band's classic early singles ('The Drowners', 'Metal Mickey', 'Animal Nitrate'). Closer to the brazen pop tease of T. Rex than to the kooky space-boy languor of *Hunky Dory* Bowie, it was a tragicomic love letter to the legions of confused, penniless, mascara-smudged teenagers who peopled singer Brett Anderson's lyrics – '*the litter on the breeze/the lovers on the streets*'.

Four years after the 'bisexual man' confession, I asked Anderson if it still applied to him. 'It was one of those statements which didn't sum up what I wanted to say as pithily as I'd hoped,' he replied. 'All I really wanted to say at the time was that I, as a person, try to be as open to everyone as I can. I'm not interested in just one segment of people. I feel pretty much that I can be anybody. One of the things that depresses me about music nowadays is that it's made for certain people, or for certain markets. It's so closed off and it's got so little love in it. I always wanted to be more than one thing, whereas a lot of bands now just look like cartoons to me. You get these ridiculous sides that you're supposed to take: I'm always being asked in Britain, 'Are you with the thugs or with the ponces?' And it's like, you can be both.'

Cardiff, December 1997. Less than three weeks after being arrested on suspicion of harbouring child pornography, the fifty-six-year-old Gary

Glitter is proceeding with his annual Christmas tour of Britain. The tour bears the unfortunate name 'A Night Out with the Boys (Could This be the Last Time?)'

Some ticket-holders have (unsuccessfully) requested refunds, but the Glitter faithful are undeterred and pour into the city's International Arena. Here, cheerfully defiant and as spectacular as ever of tonsure, the former Paul Raven gives an invigorating two-hour performance of his classic glam hits. And when it's all over he leaves the stage to the sound of 'Always Look on the Bright Side of Life'. He will wait three months to learn whether or not the police intend to press criminal charges.[7] 'The man's a hero,' protested a Welshman in a somewhat feeble glitter costume outside the arena. 'I'm behind him 100 per cent.'

'Are you ready for your good memories of Gary Glitter, *circa* 1984?' Simon Frith wrote presciently in 1973. Who knew the memories would linger on so long?

7 In March 1998, Glitter was charged with 50 counts involving child pornography in Bristol. As this book was going to press, Glitter was due to appear before magistrates on 18 May.

the greatest glam home tape in the world . . . ever

1 T. Rex: 'Ride a White Swan' (1970)
2 Alice Cooper: '(I'm) Eighteen' (1971)
3 T. Rex: 'Get It On' (1971)
4 David Bowie: 'Queen Bitch' (1971)
5 T. Rex: 'Metal Guru' (1972)
6 David Bowie: 'Ziggy Stardust' (1972)
7 Mott the Hoople: 'All the Young Dudes' (1972)
8 Roxy Music: 'Virginia Plain' (1972)
9 Gary Glitter: 'Rock and Roll Part 2' (1972)
10 Lou Reed: 'Walk on the Wild Side' (1972)
11 The Sweet: 'Ballroom Blitz' (1973)
12 Roxy Music: 'Do the Strand' (1973)
13 Iggy & the Stooges: 'Gimme Danger' (1973)
14 New York Dolls: 'Jet Boy' (1973)
15 Jobriath: 'I'maman' (1973)
16 Cockney Rebel: 'Sebastian' (1973)
17 Roxy Music: 'Street Life' (1973)
18 Queen: 'Killer Queen' (1974)
19 Eno: 'Needle's in the Camel's Eye' (1974)
20 Mick Ronson: 'Hey Ma, Get Papa' (1974)
21 The Sweet: 'Teenage Rampage' (1974)
22 David Bowie: 'Rebel Rebel' (1974)
23 Cockney Rebel: 'Tumbling Down' (1974)
24 T. Rex: 'Teenage Dream' (1974)
25 Alice Cooper: 'Teenage Lament '74' (1974)
26 Sparks: 'This Town Ain't Big Enough for Both of Us' (1974)
27 Mott the Hoople: 'Saturday Gigs' (1974)
28 T. Rex: 'Dandy in the Underworld' (1977)
29 Prince: 'Glam Slam' (1988)
30 Suede: 'Trash' (1996)

select sources

Bockris, Victor, *Lou Reed: The Biography* (London: Vintage, 1995)

– *The Life and Death of Andy Warhol* (New York: Bantam, 1989)

Bowie, Angela, with Patrick Carr, *Backstage Passes* (London: Orion, 1992)

Boy George, with Spencer Bright, *Take It Like a Man* (London: Pan, 1995)

Bracewell, Michael, *England is Mine: Pop Life in Albion, from Wilde to Goldie* (London: HarperCollins, 1997)

Bruce, Michael, with Billy James, *No More Mr Nice Guy: The Inside Story of the Alice Cooper Group* (London: SAF Publishing, 1996)

Cato, Philip, *Crash Course for the Ravers: A Glam Odyssey* (Lockerbie: S. T. Publishing, 1997)

Chapman, Rob, 'They Came from Planet Bacofoil: Roxy Music', *Mojo*, December 1995

Cochrane, Rob, 'Jobriath: The Queen of Rock and Roll,' unpublished, 1997

Core, Phillip, *Camp: The Lie That Tells the Truth* (New York: Delilah, 1984)

County, Jayne, *Man Enough to be a Woman* (London: Serpent's Tail, 1995)

Dalton, David, *The Rolling Stones: the First Twenty Years* (London: Thames, 1981)

Dellio, Phil, and Scott Woods, *I Wanna be Sedated: Pop Music in the Seventies* (Toronto: Sound and Vision, 1992)

Des Barres, Pamela, *Rock Bottom: Dark Moments in Music Babylon* (New York: St Martin's Press, 1996)

Du Noyer, Paul, 'Marc Bolan: The Man Who Would be King', *Mojo*, October 1997

Edwards, Henry, and Tony Zanetta, *Stardust: The Life and Times of David Bowie* (London: Michael Joseph, 1986)

Fisher, Ben, 'But Boy Could He Play Guitar: Mick Ronson', *Mojo*, October 1997

Frame, Pete, *The Complete Family Trees* (London: Omnibus, 1992)

Garber, Marjorie, *Vested Interests: Cross Dressing and Cultural Anxiety* (London: Routledge, 1992)

Garratt, Sheryl, 'Androgynous Heart-throbs: Confessions of a Teenage Bay City Rollers Fan', *Collusion*, 2, July–September 1982

Gillett, Charlie (ed.), *The Beat Goes On: The Rock File Reader* (London: Pluto, 1996)

Gimarc, George, *Punk Diary 1970–1979* (London: Vintage, 1994)

Glitter, Gary, with Lloyd Bradley, *Leader: The Autobiography of Gary Glitter* (London: Ebury Press, 1991)

Goldman, Albert, *Sound Bites* (New York: Turtle Bay, 1992)

Hebdidge, Dick, *Subculture: The Meaning of Style* (London: Methuen, 1979)

Heylin, Clinton, *From the Velvets to the Voidoids: A Pre-Punk History for a Post-Punk World* (Harmondsworth: Penguin, 1993)

Hodkinson, Mark, *Queen: The Early Years* (London: Omnibus, 1995)

Hoskyns, Barney, *Waiting for the Sun: Strange Days, Weird Scenes and the Sound of Los Angeles* (Harmondsworth: Viking, 1996)

Hunter, Ian, *Diary of a Rock 'n' Roll Star* (London: Independent Music Press, 1996)

Kent, Nick, *The Dark Stuff* (Harmondsworth: Penguin, 1994)

Koch, Stephen, *Stargazer: Andy Warhol's World and His Films* (London: Calder and Boyars, 1973)

Lendt, C. K., *Kiss and Sell: The Making of a Supergroup* (New York: Billboard Books, 1997)

Levy, Arthur, interview with Iggy Pop about *Raw Power* (booklet accompanying *Raw Power* remix CD, 1997)

Loud, Lance, 'Los Angeles 1972–1974: Glam Rock Loses Its Virginity', *Details*, July 1992

Loud, Lance, Kristian Hoffman and Suzan Colon, 'Mad Max's', *Details*, November 1995

McCormack, Ed, 'The Gold Lamé Dream of Bette Midler', *Rolling Stone*, 15 February 1973

McNeil, Legs, and Gillian, McCain, *Please Kill Me!: The Uncensored Oral History of Punk Rock* (New York, Grove Press, 1996)

McRobbie, Angela (ed.), *Zoot Suits and Second-Hand Dresses: An Anthology of Fashion and Music* (London: Macmillan Education, 1989)

Morley, Paul, 'Marc Bolan: A Stitch in Time', *New Musical Express*, 20 September 1980

Morrissey, Steven, *The New York Dolls* (Todmorden: Babylon Books, 1981)

Murray, Charles Shaar, *Shots from the Hip* (Harmondsworth: Penguin, 1991)

Paglia, Camille, *Sexual Personae: Art and Decadence from Nefertiti to Emily Dickinson* (New Haven: Yale University Press, 1990)

Parsons, Tony, et al., David Bowie special, *Arena*, Spring/Summer 1993

Paytress, Mark, *Marc Bolan: 20th Century Boy* (London: Sidgwick & Jackson, 1996)

Reynolds, Simon, and Joy Press, *The Sex Revolts: Gender, Rebellion, and Rock 'n' Roll* (London: Serpent's Tail, 1995)

Rimmer, Dave, *Like Punk Never Happened: Culture Club and the New Pop* (London: Faber and Faber, 1985)

Rougvie, Jeff, booklet accompanying 1990 Rykodisc reissue of David Bowie's *The Rise and Fall of Ziggy Stardust and the Spiders from Mars*

Savage, Jon, 'Androgyny: Confused Chromosomes and Camp Followers', *The Face*, June 1982, included in *Time Travel* (London:Chatto & Windus, 1996)

Sinclair, Paul, *Electric Warrior: The Marc Bolan Story* (London: Omnibus, 1982)

Singer, June, *Androgyny: Toward a New Theory of Sexuality* (New York: Anchor Press, 1976)

Sontag, Susan, 'Notes on Camp', in *Against Interpretation* (New York: Delta, 1978)

Studer, Wayne, *Rock on the Wild Side: Gay Male Images in Popular Music of the Rock Era* (San Francisco: Leyland/Turnaround, 1994)

Sutherland, Steve, 'One Day, Son, All This Could Be Yours . . .', a conversation between David Bowie and Brett Anderson, *New Musical Express*, 20 March 1993

Tamm, Eric, *Brian Eno: His Music and the Vertical Color of Sound* (Boston: Faber and Faber, 1989)

Thomson, Elizabeth, and David Gutman, *The Bowie Companion* (New York: Da Capo, 1996)

Tremlett, George, *David Bowie: Living on the Brink* (New York: Carroll & Graf, 1996)

Vermorel, Fred and Judy, *Starlust: The Secret Fantasies of Fans* (London: Comet, 1995)

Warhol, Andy, and Pat, Hackett, *POPism* (New York: Harcourt Brace Jovanovich, 1980)

Wale, Michael, *Vox Pop: Profiles of the Pop Process* (London: Harrap, 1972)

Walker, John, 'Framing Dionysus: The Gutter-Dandy in Western Culture', unpublished dissertation, University of Toronto

Williams, Richard, 'Roxy Music: Melody Maker Band Breakdown', *Melody Maker*, 29 July 1972

Films: *Born to Boogie*, *Slade in Flame*, *Stardust*, D. A. Pennebaker's film of the last Ziggy Stardust concert, the Marc Bolan documentary *Dandy in the Underworld*, the 1988 videos *Glam Rock* and *Glam Rock II*, *The Decline of Western Civilization Part 2: The Metal Years*, and Bob Gruen's New York Dolls film *Looking for a Kiss*.

index

Figures in italics refer to picture captions.